LANGUAGE A
Dorothy S. Stri
Donna E. Alvermann and
ADVISORY BOARD: Richard Allingtc
Anne Haas Dyson, Carole Edelsky, Mary J.

Widening the Lens: Integrating Multiple Approaches to Support Adolescent Literacy
DEBORAH VRIEND VAN DUINEN & ERICA R. HAMILTON

Connecting Equity, Literacy, and Language: Pathways Toward Advocacy-Focused Teaching
ALTHIER M. LAZAR, KAITLIN K. MORAN, & SHOSHANNA EDWARDS-ALEXANDER

Writing Instruction for Success in College and in the Workplace
CHARLES A. MACARTHUR & ZOI A. PHILIPPAKOS

Black Immigrant Literacies: Intersections of Race, Language, and Culture in the Classroom
PATRIANN SMITH

Teens Choosing to Read: Fostering Social, Emotional, and Intellectual Growth Through Books
GAY IVEY & PETER JOHNSTON

Critical Encounters in Secondary English: Teaching Literary Theory to Adolescents, 4th Edition
DEBORAH APPLEMAN

Reading With Purpose: Selecting and Using Children's Literature for Inquiry and Engagement
ERIKA THULIN DAWES, KATIE EGAN CUNNINGHAM, GRACE ENRIQUEZ, & MARY ANN CAPPIELLO

Core Practices for Teaching Multilingual Students: Humanizing Pedagogies for Equity
MEGAN MADIGAN PEERCY, JOHANNA M. TIGERT, & DAISY E. FREDRICKS

Bringing Sports Culture to the English Classroom: An Interest-Driven Approach to Literacy Instruction
LUKE RODESILER

Culturally Sustaining Literacy Pedagogies: Honoring Students' Heritages, Literacies, and Languages
SUSAN CHAMBERS CANTRELL, DORIS WALKER-DALHOUSE, & ALTHIER M. LAZAR, EDS.

Curating a Literacy Life: Student-Centered Learning With Digital Media
WILLIAM KIST

Understanding the Transnational Lives and Literacies of Immigrant Children
JUNGMIN KWON

The Administration and Supervision of Literacy Programs, 6th Edition
SHELLEY B. WEPNER & DIANA J. QUATROCHE, EDS.

Writing the School House Blues: Literacy, Equity, and Belonging in a Child's Early Schooling
ANNE HAAS DYSON

Playing With Language: Improving Elementary Reading Through Metalinguistic Awareness
MARCY ZIPKE

Restorative Literacies: Creating a Community of Care in Schools
DEBORAH L. WOLTER

Compose Our World: Project-Based Learning in Secondary English Language Arts
ALISON G. BOARDMAN, ANTERO GARCIA, BRIDGET DALTON, & JOSEPH L. POLMAN

Digitally Supported Disciplinary Literacy for Diverse K-5 Classrooms
JAMIE COLWELL, AMY HUTCHISON, & LINDSAY WOODWARD

The Reading Turn-Around with Emergent Bilinguals: A Five-Part Framework for Powerful Teaching and Learning (Grades K-6)
AMANDA CLAUDIA WAGER, LANE W. CLARKE, & GRACE ENRIQUEZ

Race, Justice, and Activism in Literacy Instruction
VALERIE KINLOCH, TANJA BURKHARD, & CARLOTTA PENN, EDS.

Letting Go of Literary Whiteness: Antiracist Literature Instruction for White Students
CARLIN BORSHEIM-BLACK & SOPHIA TATIANA SARIGIANIDES

The Vulnerable Heart of Literacy: Centering Trauma as Powerful Pedagogy
ELIZABETH DUTRO

Amplifying the Curriculum: Designing Quality Learning Opportunities for English Learners
AÍDA WALQUI & GEORGE C. BUNCH, EDS.

Arts Integration in Diverse K-5 Classrooms: Cultivating Literacy Skills and Conceptual Understanding
LIANE BROUILLETTE

Translanguaging for Emergent Bilinguals: Inclusive Teaching in the Linguistically Diverse Classroom
DANLING FU, XENIA HADJIOANNOU, & XIAODI ZHOU

Before Words: Wordless Picture Books and the Development of Reading in Young Children
JUDITH T. LYSAKER

Seeing the Spectrum: Teaching English Language Arts to Adolescents with Autism
ROBERT ROZEMA

A Think-Aloud Approach to Writing Assessment: Analyzing Process and Product with Adolescent Writers
SARAH W. BECK

"We've Been Doing It Your Way Long Enough": Choosing the Culturally Relevant Classroom
JANICE BAINES, CARMEN TISDALE, & SUSI LONG

Summer Reading: Closing the Rich/Poor Reading Achievement Gap, 2nd Edition
RICHARD L. ALLINGTON & ANNE MCGILL-FRANZEN, EDS.

Educating for Empathy: Literacy Learning and Civic Engagement
NICOLE MIRRA

Preparing English Learners for College and Career: Lessons from Successful High Schools
MARÍA SANTOS ET AL.

continued

For volumes in the NCRLL Collection (edited by JoBeth Allen and Donna E. Alvermann), the Practitioners Bookshelf Series (edited by Celia Genishi and Donna E. Alvermann), and other titles in this series, please visit www.tcpress.com

Language and Literacy Series, *continued*

Reading the Rainbow
CAITLIN L. RYAN & JILL M. HERMANN-WILMARTH

Educating Emergent Bilinguals, 2nd Ed.
OFELIA GARCÍA & JO ANNE KLEIFGEN

Social Justice Literacies in the English Classroom
ASHLEY S. BOYD

Remixing Multiliteracies
FRANK SERAFINI & ELISABETH GEE, EDS.

Culturally Sustaining Pedagogies
DJANGO PARIS & H. SAMY ALIM, EDS.

Choice and Agency in the Writing Workshop
FRED L. HAMEL

Assessing Writing, Teaching Writers
MARY ANN SMITH & SHERRY SEALE SWAIN

The Teacher-Writer
CHRISTINE M. DAWSON

Every Young Child a Reader
SHARAN A. GIBSON & BARBARA MOSS

"You Gotta BE the Book," 3rd Ed.
JEFFREY D. WILHELM

Personal Narrative, Revised
BRONWYN CLARE LAMAY

Inclusive Literacy Teachings
LORI HELMAN ET AL.

The Vocabulary Book, 2nd Ed.
MICHAEL F. GRAVES

Reading, Writing, and Talk
MARIANA SOUTO-MANNING & JESSICA MARTELL

Go Be a Writer!
CANDACE R. KUBY & TARA GUTSHALL RUCKER

Partnering with Immigrant Communities
GERALD CAMPANO ET AL.

Teaching Outside the Box but Inside the Standards
BOB FECHO ET AL., EDS.

Literacy Leadership in Changing Schools
SHELLEY B. WEPNER ET AL.

Literacy Theory as Practice
LARA J. HANDSFIELD

Literacy and History in Action
THOMAS M. MCCANN ET AL.

Pose, Wobble, Flow
ANTERO GARCIA & CINDY O'DONNELL-ALLEN

Newsworthy
ED MADISON

Engaging Writers with Multigenre Research Projects
NANCY MACK

Teaching Transnational Youth
ALLISON SKERRETT

Uncommonly Good Ideas
SANDRA MURPHY & MARY ANN SMITH

The One-on-One Reading and Writing Conference
JENNIFER BERNE & SOPHIE C. DEGENER

Transforming Talk into Text
THOMAS M. MCCANN

Educating Literacy Teachers Online
LANE W. CLARKE & SUSAN WATTS-TAFFEE

WHAM! Teaching with Graphic Novels Across the Curriculum
WILLIAM G. BROZO ET AL.

Critical Literacy in the Early Childhood Classroom
CANDACE R. KUBY

Inspiring Dialogue
MARY M. JUZWIK ET AL.

Reading the Visual
FRANK SERAFINI

ReWRITING the Basics
ANNE HAAS DYSON

Writing Instruction That Works
ARTHUR N. APPLEBEE ET AL.

Literacy Playshop
KAREN E. WOHLWEND

Critical Media Pedagogy
ERNEST MORRELL ET AL.

A Search Past Silence
DAVID E. KIRKLAND

The ELL Writer
CHRISTINA ORTMEIER-HOOPER

Reading in a Participatory Culture
HENRY JENKINS ET AL., EDS.

Teaching Vocabulary to English Language Learners
MICHAEL F. GRAVES ET AL.

Bridging Literacy and Equity
ALTHIER M. LAZAR ET AL.

Reading Time
CATHERINE COMPTON-LILLY

Interrupting Hate
MOLLIE V. BLACKBURN

Playing Their Way into Literacies
KAREN E. WOHLWEND

Teaching Literacy for Love and Wisdom
JEFFREY D. WILHELM & BRUCE NOVAK

Urban Literacies
VALERIE KINLOCH, ED.

Bedtime Stories and Book Reports
CATHERINE COMPTON-LILLY & STUART GREENE, EDS.

Envisioning Knowledge
JUDITH A. LANGER

Envisioning Literature, 2nd Ed.
JUDITH A. LANGER

Artifactual Literacies
KATE PAHL & JENNIFER ROWSELL

Change Is Gonna Come
PATRICIA A. EDWARDS ET AL.

Harlem on Our Minds
VALERIE KINLOCH

Children, Language, and Literacy
CELIA GENISHI & ANNE HAAS DYSON

Children's Language
JUDITH WELLS LINDFORS

Storytime
LAWRENCE R. SIPE

Widening the Lens

Integrating Multiple Approaches to Support Adolescent Literacy

Deborah Vriend Van Duinen
and Erica R. Hamilton

Foreword by Julie Bell

TEACHERS COLLEGE PRESS
TEACHERS COLLEGE | COLUMBIA UNIVERSITY
NEW YORK AND LONDON

Published by Teachers College Press,® 1234 Amsterdam Avenue, New York, NY 10027

Copyright © 2024 by Teachers College, Columbia University

Front cover design by Peter Donahue. Photos by (clockwise from top): Ridofranz; Prostock-Studio; TuiPhotoengineer; Anna Stills; Mediaphotos; Rawpixel; Kerkez; and Hero Images, all via iStock by Getty Images.

All rights reserved. No part of this publication may be reproduced or transmitted in any form or by any means, electronic or mechanical, including photocopy, or any information storage and retrieval system, without permission from the publisher. For reprint permission and other subsidiary rights requests, please contact Teachers College Press, Rights Dept.: tcpressrights@tc.columbia.edu

Library of Congress Cataloging-in-Publication Data

Names: Van Duinen, Deborah Vriend, author. | Hamilton, Erica R., author.
Title: Widening the lens : integrating multiple approaches to support adolescent literacy / Deborah Vriend Van Duinen and Erica R. Hamilton.
Description: New York : Teachers College Press, [2024] | Series: Language and literacy series | Includes bibliographical references and index.
Identifiers: LCCN 2023040065 (print) | LCCN 2023040066 (ebook) | ISBN 9780807769027 (paper : acid-free paper) | ISBN 9780807769034 (hardcover : acid-free paper) | ISBN 9780807782057 (ebook)
Subjects: LCSH: Reading (Secondary) | Literacy—Study and teaching (Secondary) | Content area reading—Study and teaching (Secondary) | Language arts—Correlation with content subjects. | High school teachers—Training of.
Classification: LCC LB1632 .V34 2024 (print) | LCC LB1632 (ebook) | DDC 418/.40712—dc23/eng/20231103
LC record available at https://lccn.loc.gov/2023040065
LC ebook record available at https://lccn.loc.gov/2023040066

ISBN 978-0-8077-6902-7 (paper)
ISBN 978-0-8077-6903-4 (hardcover)
ISBN 978-0-8077-8205-7 (ebook)

Printed on acid-free paper
Manufactured in the United States of America

*To our families, who are our best teachers,
and to secondary teachers who show up
for students every day*

Contents

Foreword *Julie Bell*	xi
Acknowledgments	xv
Introduction	1
Adolescent Literacy	2
Theories	2
A Widened Lens Metaphor and a "Yes, And" Approach	3
1. Concepts, Definitions, and Beliefs	7
Literacy	7
Literacy Instruction	9
(Re)Defining Adolescence and Adolescents	10
(Re)Defining Adolescent Literacy	13
"Yes, And" Approach	14
Moving Forward	25
2. Adolescents' Literacy Skills	27
Three Approaches to Literacy Instruction	28
Reading and Writing Skills	31
Developing and Supporting Adolescents' Reading and Writing Proficiency	41
"Yes, And" Approach to Adolescents' Reading and Writing Skills	43
Moving Forward	44

3. Adolescents' Literacy Contexts and Practices   45

Context   46

Literacy in Context   46

Adolescents' Literacy Practices in Context   53

Acknowledging and Valuing Adolescents' Literacy Contexts and Practices   55

Integrating Adolescents' Literacy Contexts and Practices   57

"Yes, And" Approach to Adolescents' Literacy Contexts and Practices   59

Moving Forward   60

4. Identifying and Using Texts   61

Identifying Texts   61

Considering the Complexity of Texts   64

Using Texts for Instructional Purposes   73

"Yes, And" Approach to Identifying and Using Texts   76

Moving Forward   77

5. Literacy Strategies Across Subject Areas   79

Literacy Skill Development   79

Using Literacy Strategies to Support Adolescents' Literacy Skill Development   83

Using Literacy Strategies for Instructional Purposes   93

"Yes, And" Approach to Using Literacy Strategies Across Subject Areas   96

Moving Forward   97

6. Disciplinary Literacy Instruction   99

Disciplinary Literacy   99

Disciplinary Literacy Instruction   101

"Yes, And" Approach to Disciplinary Literacy Instruction and Literacy Strategies   113

Moving Forward   114

Conclusion	**117**
Key Takeaways: "Yes, And" Considerations	118
Moving Forward	119
References	**121**
Index	**131**
About the Authors	**137**

Foreword

In one of my graduate courses, I was tasked with writing a definition of literacy. Even as a former high school English teacher, I found the task somewhat challenging; I can only imagine how my colleagues who came from other backgrounds and disciplines felt. The following was my initial definition:

> Literacy is part of everyday life. There is no escaping it. Literacy means communicating in many different forms, including reading, writing, and speaking (among others). The ways in which people are literate are shaped by the culture in which they live.

By the end of the course, my definition was more nuanced, influenced by the reading, writing, and discussions we had during the semester. Based largely on Moje and Luke's (2009) review of research about literacy and identity, the following was my revised definition: Literacy is social, varied, individual, evolving, and "more than a set of autonomous skills" (p. 416). Now, as a faculty member who works with preservice and in-service teachers, I endeavor to help my students understand and apply these nuances within K–12 education, which is critical to advancing learners' growth and development. In this book, Deborah Vriend Van Duinen and Erica R. Hamilton invite readers to broaden their understanding of literacy to support teaching and learning in secondary classrooms across all disciplines. As they note, adolescent literacy is important, not just for English Language Arts teachers, but for *all* preservice and in-service teachers because literacy is key for all learners across disciplines.

Through a widened lens metaphor, the authors explore literacy-based theories, while also applying a "yes, and" approach borrowed from improvisational comedy. Many teacher educators, including me, have encountered preservice teachers who initially define the term *literacy* simply as the ability to read. Van Duinen and Hamilton identify this as one of seven commonly held beliefs about literacy that they use the "yes, and" method to expand. For example, the "yes, and" version is, "Literacy is the ability to read, write, speak, listen, and represent." Following the commonly held beliefs, the authors address various approaches to literacy instruction.

Rather than declaring one approach the best way to foster adolescent literacy development, the authors use their widened lens metaphor to describe three key approaches: science of reading, whole language, and balanced literacy. Their descriptions help readers situate themselves in the field and determine which parts of each approach will best serve their students.

Through this book, readers are encouraged to expand their conceptions of *literacy, adolescence, adolescents,* and *adolescent literacy.* Maintaining an asset-based view of adolescents throughout, the authors acknowledge learners' interests and literacy practices outside of school, noting ways teachers can utilize these literacy practices to contribute to students' academic literacy development across disciplines. Bolstered by research and personal examples, Van Duinen and Hamilton explore various approaches to supporting adolescents' literacy development through purposeful instruction, text selection, and employing content area and disciplinary literacy strategies in ways that value students' personal literacy practices and expand their academic development.

For many years, scholars have debated which type of strategies best support student learning: general content area literacy strategies (e.g., Fagella-Luby et al., 2012) or specific disciplinary literacy strategies (e.g., Shanahan & Shanahan, 2008). Van Duinen and Hamilton set their text apart from other books about adolescent literacy instruction by including examples and strategies from both content area reading and disciplinary literacy. This "both and" or "radical center" (Brozo et al., 2013) approach is yet another reason this book will be appealing to preservice and in-service teachers of all subjects, as well as teacher educators.

Widening the Lens: Integrating Multiple Approaches to Support Adolescent Literacy invites teacher educators, in-service teachers, and preservice teachers to reflect on and expand their understanding of adolescent literacy pedagogies and practices. Doing so empowers readers to address the diverse needs of their students. Rooted in research and the authors' own experiences and expertise, this is an accessible book that includes examples, resources, practical applications, and questions to consider. Centered on how to support adolescents' literacy development within and across subject areas at the secondary level, this is a book I wish I had owned as a preservice teacher and in my early years of teaching, and it is a book I'm excited to share with the preservice and in-service teachers I work with now.

Julie Bell
Associate Professor of Teacher Education
University of Nebraska at Omaha

REFERENCES

Moje, E. B. & Luke, A. (2009). Literacy and identity: Examining the metaphors in history and contemporary research. *Reading Research Quarterly, 44*(4), 415–437.

Brozo, W. G., Moorman, G., Meyer, C., & Stewart, T. (2013). Content area reading and disciplinary literacy: A case for the radical center. *Journal of Adolescent & Adult Literacy, 56*(5), 353–357.

Fagella-Luby, M. N., Graner, P. S., Deshler, D. D., & Drew, S. V. (2012). Building a house on sand: Why disciplinary is not sufficient to replace general strategies for adolescent learners who struggle. *Topics in Language Disorders, 32*(1), 69–84.

Shanahan, T. & Shanahan, C. (2008). Teaching disciplinary literacy to adolescents: Rethinking content-area literacy. *Harvard Educational Review, 78*(1), 40–59.

Acknowledgments

We remain grateful to all the preservice teachers we've worked with over the span of our careers and to the many in-service teachers who partner with us to support this work.

We also extend thanks to colleagues who shared feedback, including their time and expertise, as we wrote this book, specifically Dr. Anny Fritzen Case (Gonzaga University), Dr. Christine Dawson (Siena College), Dr. Elizabeth Grimm (Hope College), Dr. Min-Young Kim (University of Kansas), Dr. Laura Pardo (Hope College), and Dr. Alyssa Whitford (Hope College).

We are especially grateful to Dr. Troy Hicks (Central Michigan University), who has been instrumental throughout the process, from the very beginning, and has generously offered guidance, feedback, and mentorship.

Widening the Lens

Introduction

Literacy is a fundamental skill and remains central to many, if not most, social and economic opportunities. Literacy is also connected to various workplace demands, job security, and health outcomes (Career Outlook Data on Display, 2020; Vernon et al., 2007). For adolescents, low literacy skills are connected with high school dropout rates, health, and the school-to-prison pipeline (Winn, 2011). In other words, literacy skills matter.

In the United States, when standardized reading and writing scores are measured on state, national, and international tests (e.g., ACT, SAT, NAEP, and PISA), recent data suggest that only 34% of 8th-graders in the United States are reading at grade level (National Center for Education Statistics, 2019). Statistics for students of color and low-income students are even more dismal, with 15% of low-income, 26% of Hispanic, and 14% of Black 8th-graders reading at or higher than their grade level. These standardized test scores have led to increased attention to adolescents' literacy skills in the past 2 decades, with the language of "crisis" used (Jacobs, 2008; Salinger, 2011; Sparks, 2022). On the one hand, this increased attention has propelled advocacy and funding for adolescent literacy, resulting in many reports, research initiatives, and professional development focused on adolescent literacy (e.g., Biancarosa & Snow, 2006; Graham & Perin, 2007; Heller & Greenleaf, 2007; National Institute for Literacy, 2007). This has led to more awareness and acceptance of the importance of all secondary teachers being equipped and empowered to support their adolescent students' literacy development in and across subject areas. This increased attention to adolescent literacy has also resulted in many different (and, at times, competing and conflicting) approaches to adolescent literacy instruction. For example, one approach may rely on predetermined texts and skills-centered instruction whereas another emphasizes student choice and exploration related to texts and skills. While different approaches can be used to support adolescent literacy development, these differences can be confusing to beginning teachers because of their differing purposes, outcomes, and underlying assertions. One approach rarely tells the whole story or provides the full picture. Much more needs to be considered.

ADOLESCENT LITERACY

In this book, we use the term "adolescent literacy" to refer to the ways learners, ages 10 to 18, acquire and use specific knowledge for specific purposes in a given context. For secondary teachers, supporting adolescents' literacy development means connecting what students learn in the classroom to relevant issues and experiences in their lives and the contexts in which they live and work, including their homes, families, houses of worship, places of employment, and communities. As a result, adolescent literacy development and instruction must focus on skill and knowledge development and how adolescents make sense of their worlds.

As teacher educators, we've explored many ways to introduce and articulate key ideas connected to adolescent literacy to the beginning teachers we've worked with. Over the years, we've used a variety of approaches, texts, and activities in the undergraduate and graduate adolescent literacy courses we've taught. We've learned a lot from these experiences and from the many beginning teachers we've been privileged to work with. This book is the result of what we've learned and what we continue to learn.

Whereas many other (excellent) books explore particular aspects of adolescent literacy, this book provides a much-needed big-picture view of the field. We've written this book for preservice teachers and those new to the profession who may not yet have much experience working in secondary classrooms. This book is also for educators working to make sense of the many and sometimes competing adolescent literacy initiatives, research studies, and instructional strategies. As such, our goal is to provide an overview of important aspects of adolescent literacy that impact teaching at the secondary level. In this book we identify specific literacy skills, explore the importance of literacy contexts and practices, examine literacy strategies across content areas, and discuss disciplinary literacy instruction. The result is a succinct, holistic, and integrated approach to learning about and understanding the complexities of adolescent literacy instruction and assessment.

THEORIES

Theories (i.e., ideas and beliefs) about teaching and learning matter, and learning about theories can help educators reflect on what they believe to be true about teaching and learning, including what they do (i.e., practice) and why they do it (i.e., pedagogy). We all have theories about things that inform our thinking and actions. In our personal lives, the theories we hold, implicit or explicit, influence our thoughts and behavior. As educators, we also draw on implicit and explicit theories that inform our work. For example, suppose a teacher theorizes that all students can learn and achieve at a high level. If so, this teacher will teach and interact with adolescents differently than if they believe only some students can learn and achieve at a high level (Dweck, 2008). As a result, it's important, particularly when being introduced to new ideas and theories, to identify and understand the beliefs that inform them. In fact, all teachers should know and understand the different theories that guide their pedagogies and practices.

It's important to know where various literacy initiatives come from and what perspectives and theories they might represent. Knowing the context and subsequent development of various strategies and literacy approaches offers teachers a broader, more robust understanding of pedagogies and practices, including their possibilities and limitations. Adolescent literacy instruction, like reading and writing instruction in general, has a particular historical and cultural context and continues to evolve as new research develops. Tracing the development of this research gives us a clearer view of how this field has developed and changed, including the terms used within the field. These changes in terminology over time might not seem significant, but they reveal new knowledge developments and shifts in thinking. Recognizing these shifts is important because it helps situate new initiatives and approaches within their historical context.

Like other professions and professionals, education systems and educators' pedagogies and practices are situated in multiple historical and cultural contexts. As teachers of adolescents, our pedagogies and practices come out of and respond to particular perspectives, situations, and time periods. This knowledge, in turn, can support our decisions about what strategies and approaches we choose to use and implement with our adolescent students.

A WIDENED LENS METAPHOR AND A "YES, AND" APPROACH

In their 2004 book *Print Literacy Development*, Purcell-Gates et al. use the metaphor of a widened lens to explain the importance of integrating various theories to support students' learning. Rather than dichotomously positioning literacy theories directly against one another, they envisioned these theories not as independent and incommensurable but as existing within a nested relationship. This concept of a nested relationship and the importance of seeing how different theories could work together immediately resonated with us because of how it clearly frames and creates room for different theories to map onto and inform one another. We started using this widened lens metaphor with our undergraduate and graduate students when we discussed literacy theories. From there, we began to think about how a widened lens metaphor might also help approach other topics and aspects of adolescent literacy development and instruction.

Given the multifaceted nature of adolescents, literacy, and adolescent literacy instruction, it's important for beginning teachers to have a big-picture view of the factors, concepts, theories, and practices that represent adolescent literacy. Secondary teachers and their students are best served when drawing on multiple theories and research-based practices. This results in a more robust understanding of literacy development in and across subject areas, which in turn positively impacts teachers' pedagogy and practice and students' learning. As teacher educators, former teachers, and researchers in the field of adolescent literacy, we know it can be easy to focus on one new approach or theory related to adolescent literacy, but we are better served when we understand the larger landscape and how pedagogies and practices interact with and respond to each other. When we rely too heavily on any one theory or approach related to adolescent literacy development and instruction, we lose the ability to more deeply and comprehensively understand how to best serve and meet adolescents' literacy needs.

As we experimented with using a widened lens metaphor with the beginning and experienced teachers we worked with, we found it helpful to introduce the concept of "yes, and" from improv comedy as a way of helping teachers understand what it means to apply a widened lens to one's pedagogy and practice in secondary classroom settings. In improv comedy, one of the key rules is that an actor must not only accept what is given but also build upon it (Salinsky & Frances-White, 2017). For example, when an actor says, "I'm a mechanic," another actor might follow up with, "Yes, and I'm a car owner with a brand-new car that has an engine that keeps overheating." From there the actors are expected to continue accepting and building on what each other says. The result of a "yes, and" approach is a codeveloped narrative that takes a present idea or reality and expands it (Pories, 2014; Salinsky & Frances-White, 2017).

A "yes, and" approach has been successfully applied in multiple fields beyond improv comedy, demonstrating the power of building on established ideas, suggestions, and assertions (Pories, 2014). Applying the approach within the adolescent literacy field provides teachers with a framework for understanding, situating, and drawing from different theories, practices, and approaches rather than focusing solely on one. As we'll see in chapter 1, there are several commonly held beliefs about adolescent literacy. When we apply a "yes, and" approach to these commonly held beliefs about adolescents, literacy, and adolescent literacy instruction, we expand our understanding and increase our capacity for supporting and serving adolescent learners.

This book invites readers to widen their lens on the topic of adolescent literacy by exploring salient and relevant topics connected with adolescent literacy and their application in the classroom. Navigating the complicated and complex terrain of adolescent literacy isn't easy. Having a big-picture view is helpful and necessary as beginning teachers encounter and are encouraged to implement many different adolescent literacy initiatives, programs, curricula, and professional development opportunities. Within this widened lens of adolescent literacy, this book also invites readers to adopt a "yes, and" approach by considering how the topics and their corresponding theories, approaches, and practices related to adolescent literacy might inform and/or work in concert with each other.

In each chapter, we focus on one aspect of adolescent literacy and outline key concepts, terms, and ideas related to it. We share examples and relevant research to support teachers' understanding of adolescent literacy, including practical applications. To guide readers, at the beginning of each chapter, we highlight key terms and definitions within that chapter. After each chapter, we pose questions that can be discussed in small groups and/or reflected on individually.

CHAPTER 1

Concepts, Definitions, and Beliefs

KEY TERMS

Adolescent: a learner between the ages of 10 and 18
Literacy: how humans acquire and use specific knowledge for specific purposes in a given context
Pedagogy: the study and understanding of how knowledge and skills are taught in learning settings, including specific approaches, methods, and strategies
Practice: the approaches, methods, and strategies teachers use when teaching

LITERACY

As noted in the introduction, "literacy" is a widely used term that means different things to different people. Beginning secondary teachers have heard this term throughout their lives—in newspaper headlines, popular culture texts, school contexts, and government initiatives, to name a few. So, when hearing "literacy" in the context of something they need to do with their adolescent students in different subject areas, it can be challenging for beginning teachers to know their role in supporting students' literacy development.

Defining Literacy

The term "literacy" is used to refer to the act of learning to read and write, and by extension, the act of learning to decode and encode words and becoming fluent with reading and writing print-based texts. For example, the *Oxford English Dictionary* defines literacy as "the quality, condition, or state of being literate; the ability to read and write." The term is also used to describe school-based learning opportunities and the types of engagement with texts that happen in school. When the word "literacy" is used with a modifier, it is generally understood to refer to proficiency in different areas of knowledge. For example, musical literacy, digital literacy, health literacy, medical literacy, informational literacy, emotional literacy, and financial literacy can be terms used to describe "the ability to 'read' a specified subject or medium" or, more generally, competence or knowledge in a particular area." When someone is literate in any of these areas, or when they have achieved literacy in each area, it means they know a lot about and understand a particular subject. It also means being able to engage with and clearly recognize these traditions, activities, and history in spaces such as news stories, publications, social media, the arts, museums, stories, and performances.

In the field of literacy research, particularly connected to teaching and learning, the term "literacy" has been approached and studied in several ways (Fang, 2012a). Some researchers focus on cognitive approaches, looking at what happens in the brains or minds of readers. Others approach literacy with a linguistic lens, analyzing how academic language, vocabulary, and instruction focuses on words, sentences, and whole texts. Another approach, a sociocultural approach, analyzes students' various backgrounds and languages related to how learners become literate. Additionally, a critical approach foregrounds issues of power and privilege when examining and understanding literacy. Freire (2000), for example, coined the term "critical literacy," which refers to the need to "read both the word and world." Freire advocated for an understanding of literacy that involves not just reading words and comprehending the knowledge represented by those words but also the knowledge that comes with the words, specifically as a means of understanding our world as well as advocating for change.

For the purposes of this book, we define "literacy" as how humans acquire and use specific knowledge for specific purposes in a given context.

Literacy and School

In many school contexts, "literacy" is inserted in schools' visions, missions, and improvement plans. Literacy initiatives are generally focused at the elementary level and, more often than not, focus on reading support and instruction. Moreover, heated debates occur in the field of literacy instruction about how, when, what, in which order, and how long to provide systematic and explicit reading instruction. Many of these debates have become sensationalized, headline-focused, political, and overly simplified in attempts to make a particular argument. They are framed in terms of contrasts or dichotomies of good and bad.

Furthermore, many teachers as well as school and district leaders are measured by students' standardized literacy test scores. This performance indicator results in varied literacy-focused professional development for teachers at the school, district, and even state and national levels. With the expressed goal of increasing students' academic literacy—specifically their ability to read and write, much of this professional development centers on reading strategies and supports.

Concepts, Definitions, and Beliefs

There is merit to the different ways people talk about, define, and apply their understanding of literacy, including different types (e.g., cultural literacy, financial literacy, critical literacy, academic literacy). That said, these varied uses of this term can also be confusing. At times, literacy is used narrowly to describe the ability to read, which is associated with academic literacy. At other times, literacy is used in vague ways that reference knowledge within a context. To add to the possible confusion, the words "literacy," "literature," and "literary" look and sound similar and are sometimes confused.

Aspects of Literacy

When working with beginning secondary teachers, we first start with these varied understandings of literacy. We invite teachers to consider what they already know and have experienced related to the term "literacy," including when it is used with a modifier (e.g., critical literacy). This exploration encourages beginning teachers to reflect on what they've heard and how they've used this term in different contexts such as school, media outlets, conversation, and popular culture. We then use these reflections to co-construct an understanding of how the term "literacy" is used, constructed, and applied specific to adolescents. After this initial exploration, we pose questions intended to invite more complicated and nuanced conversations about various aspects of literacy:

- At what level of reading or writing is someone considered literate?
- What does it mean to be able to read, write, and communicate effectively? Who gets to decide this?
- Who is responsible for ensuring that students are literate?
- When should students learn how to read and write?
- How should students learn how to read and write?
- When thinking about texts other than books (e.g., images, audio and video recordings, web-based content), what additional literacy skills might adolescents need?

Thinking and talking together about these questions can help identify the many, and complicated, issues and underlying theories that inform our different understandings of literacy and what is involved in becoming literate.

LITERACY INSTRUCTION

In our work with beginning teachers, we also explore different approaches to literacy instruction as they relate to reading. Building on the discussions above, we follow up with questions intended to expose the complexities involved in determining best or effective instructional approaches to supporting students' literacy development:

- What literacy skills should be taught, including when, where, and how?
- Should literacy skills be taught in isolation or embedded within other experiences?
- What role might students' cultural, ethnic, racial, and socioeconomic context play in literacy instruction?
- What texts should be used to support literacy development?
- Do literacy skills look the same in different subject areas or are they different?

Responses to these questions are revealing as they identify differing ideas, perspectives, and resources. As we discuss these questions, we highlight three approaches to reading instruction: science of reading, whole language, and balanced literacy. Frequently referred to by a variety of stakeholders, these approaches reveal not only the complexities inherent in literacy instruction but also the complexities that define ongoing conversations about literacy instruction.

(RE)DEFINING ADOLESCENCE AND ADOLESCENTS

In the same way that "literacy" and "literacy instruction" are complex terms, the concept of adolescence and adolescents themselves are equally complex. Adolescence generally refers to the phase of life between childhood and adulthood, from ages 10 to 18 (World Health Organization, 2023). Many terms are used to describe this age group, including "teens," "juveniles," "young adults" and "adolescents." For our purposes in this book, we use the term "adolescent" and focus on adolescent learners in middle school and high school (grades 6–12).

Adolescence

Adolescence is a time of physical and learning growth, including many hormonal changes. Adolescents' brains continue developing as these changes occur, resulting in varied biological and behavioral changes (Harper, 2018). Adolescents' brains also experience a second round of neural plasticity, which provides additional opportunities for adolescents to develop new ways of thinking and learning about their world. Authors of the Alliance for Excellent Education's (2018) report explain that adolescence represents a stage of development in which the human brain becomes more efficient and specialized.

Concepts, Definitions, and Beliefs 11

Adolescents' learning experiences and environments in and beyond school influence when, what, and how they learn because their learning and development are directly connected. As their brains develop during this time, adolescents develop their ability to engage in adult levels of thinking and complex cognition (e.g., thinking about the future, abstract reasoning, etc.). During this time in their lives, adolescents' capacity to form memories and ascertain the accuracy of these memories continues to develop. Moreover, adolescents become more skilled at assessing their learning, including identifying what works or doesn't work well. At the same time, due to the emotional, cognitive, and physical changes they experience during their tween and teen years, we also know that adolescence is a time in which young people, compared to adults and children, experience higher risks connected to various issues (e.g., mental and behavioral health, substance and alcohol abuse, trauma, accidents). Suleiman and Dahl (2017) describe adolescents' learning experiences in this way:

> First, adolescents are highly motivated to engage in learning relevant to social relationships. They experience a profound increase in interest in engaging in social roles with peers and potential romantic partners and navigating and understanding social hierarchies and sexual and romantic behavior. Second, learning about oneself and finding one's place in social hierarchies becomes a primary motivator of early adolescent behavior. This includes an amplified salience of self-conscious emotions, including both a strong desire for acceptance, belonging, admiration, and respect, as well as increased sensitivity to feelings of rejection, disrespect, embarrassment, and humiliation. (p. 24)

Clearly, understanding the changes adolescents experience, as well as the science behind adolescents' learning and development, is crucial to effectively support adolescent learning (Alliance for Excellent Education, 2018).

As teachers and parents of adolescents ourselves, we can attest to these changes and know it's an incredible time of development, exploration, and learning. We also know that adolescents need choice, autonomy, purpose, competence, acceptance, and encouragement (Shipp, 2017). As a result, this unique time in a learner's life offers important teaching and learning opportunities, including those related to literacy.

Adolescents

It's easy to think about adolescents as having specific age- and body-dependent characteristics. In other words, it's easy to assume that adolescents act in predictable, specific, and universal ways because they are going through adolescence. Popular media such as TV shows, films, and news stories contribute to and reinforce these assumptions, including that all adolescents are hormone-driven, peer-focused, risk-taking, moody, and irresponsible. Being aware of these, often negative, assumptions about adolescents and adolescence is important because they affect "what we teach, how we teach, and even why we teach" (Sarigianides et al., 2017, p. 2). In our work with beginning teachers, we encourage them to identify popular constructions of or stereotypes about adolescents and then reflect on their own experiences as adolescents as well as those of others. These identified constructions and stereotypes fall apart during our conversations because of how diverse adolescents are in terms of their interests, experiences, and motivations.

Approaching adolescents in asset-based ways also challenges popular assumptions about this age group. Looking at what adolescents do in and out of school, it's easy to see their creativity, resilience, and talent. They are curious, motivated, and eager to learn. They participate in varied reading, writing, speaking, and listening tasks in their school settings. They engage in peer-to-peer conversations during class, offering explanations and evidence centered on their thinking and learning. They participate in in-class presentations, ones they facilitate and those offered by their peers. At times, they create and record podcast episodes and videos, which are posted to class and/or school websites. In other instances, they design and share websites related to their learning. They create graphs, tables, and drawings and generate and curate images that connect to content. They are active in physical education, learning new games and skills while interacting with peers. Moreover, they also interpret and act out scenes from plays, stories, and historical events. They also dance, perform, and play music, showcased through community events and concert performances.

In their lives outside of school, adolescents consume and create videos, blogs, and podcasts. They write and perform songs, poetry, and stories. They play video games, participate in sports and the performing arts, and engage in hobbies that have little or nothing to do with what they do in school (e.g., hunting, engine mechanics, knitting, graphic and website design, baking, sewing). Some adolescents start their own nonprofits; others participate in social influencing; while still others volunteer in their communities, provide mentoring and peer support, and participate in social justice campaigns. Clearly, the literacy skills required for these activities are sophisticated and complex. And, because adolescents have their own purposes and reasons for participating in them, they are highly motivated to do them and get better at them. And yet, many of these literacy skills are not recognized in school and/or are underutilized. Teachers can easily overlook, ignore, censor, and even devalue the many literacy experiences adolescents bring with them into school contexts. When we think about how adolescents are developing, growing, and learning, we readily acknowledge that this is a time in life unlike any other in a learner's life. This means there is a tremendous opportunity for teaching and learning at the secondary level—and this is exciting!

(RE)DEFINING ADOLESCENT LITERACY

This book centers on adolescent literacy, which we define as the ways learners, ages 10 to 18, acquire and use specific knowledge for particular purposes in a given context. Adolescent literacy differs from early literacy and adult literacy instruction and research. In other words, what works when supporting younger learners' literacy development doesn't necessarily work, or work in the same way, when it comes to adolescents. Similarly, working with adults on developing their academic literacy skills requires different understandings, strategies, and approaches as compared to working with adolescents. Adolescent literacy development occurs and needs to be supported in ways that are particular to the realities and experiences of adolescents both inside and outside of school.

In many instances, the term "adolescent literacy" is used to refer to what adolescents do in school contexts and to the ways they can be supported in developing reading and writing practices as they encounter concepts and content across the subject areas in the secondary grade levels. However, it's broader than this. Adolescent literacy also refers to the issues and experiences that matter to adolescents and that occur in all the contexts of their lives, including their homes, families, communities, houses of worship, and places of employment. As a result, adolescent literacy development and instruction must focus on how adolescents make sense of their world through how and what they read, write, speak, listen, and represent. It also needs to acknowledge and draw from the ways adolescents understand, interpret, and produce knowledge in all the contexts of their lives.

How one understands adolescents and adolescent literacy matters because there are almost always differences between a teacher who believes adolescents need to be directly engaged in their learning through regular inquiry and peer-to-peer interaction compared to a teacher who primarily employs a lecture-based approach in which students remain silent in a classroom, listening and taking notes (Simon & Kalan, 2017). These approaches stem from separate theories about teaching and learning, including how learning is best accomplished. Both approaches have merit, and both originate from collective desires to better understand humans, including addressing their learning needs, wants, and development. The intention and purposes are similar, but the conclusions and actions for how to best accomplish these are quite different.

Pedagogy and Practice

Nothing happens in a vacuum. Like other professions and professionals, systems of education and educators' pedagogies and practices are situated in multiple historical and cultural contexts. As secondary teachers, our pedagogies and practices come out of and respond to various perspectives, situations, and theories. So, understanding adolescent literacy as well as knowing the context and subsequent development of various strategies and approaches offers teachers a broader, more robust understanding. This knowledge, in turn, supports their decisions about what strategies and approaches they choose to use and implement with their adolescent students.

In the following chapters, we explore important aspects of adolescent literacy development and instruction. We start by addressing commonly held beliefs about literacy and adolescents that have surfaced in our conversations with beginning teachers over the years. These beliefs make sense to us. In fact, these commonly held beliefs provide insight and understanding into how various literacy initiatives and approaches are framed and implemented (National Council of Teachers of English [NCTE], 2007). However, these beliefs can also be limiting and limited. There's a bigger picture that exists that can lead to new connections and expanded perspectives.

"YES, AND" APPROACH

Below are some commonly held beliefs about literacy. In the introduction, we explained how the metaphor of a widened lens encourages secondary teachers to utilize a "yes, and" approach when it comes to adolescent literacy. When we apply a "yes, and" approach to these commonly held beliefs, we expand our understanding and increase our capacity for supporting and serving adolescent learners (Table 1.1).

Table 1.1. "Yes, And" Approach to Commonly Held Beliefs About Literacy

Commonly Held Beliefs About Literacy	Yes, And ...
Literacy is the ability to read	Literacy is the ability to read, write, speak, listen, and represent
Literacy refers to general skill	Literacy refers to general and specific skills
Literacy development is finite	Literacy development is ongoing
Literacy is school based	Literacy is school-, home-, and community-based
Literacy instruction is the responsibility of English Language Arts teachers	Literacy instruction is the responsibility of all teachers
Literacy instruction is one-size-fits-all	Literacy instruction is multifaceted
Literacy instruction is skills based	Literacy instruction is contextual, including skill-development aligned with different disciplines and practices

In the following seven sections we introduce each belief, explore some of the key perspectives that contribute to them, and explain why an expanded understanding is necessary and beneficial for teachers and students. In subsequent chapters, we will revisit and further explore these beliefs as they relate to important components of adolescent literacy.

Belief: Literacy Is the Ability to Read

As we've said before, it's easy to think only about reading when we think about literacy. Connected to adolescent literacy instruction, reading is important. Students' reading proficiency levels, as determined by district, state, and national assessments, gain a lot of attention in the popular media and are sometimes connected to funding decisions, staff allocations, and teacher pay. Standardized reading scores can also open or close doors for students who want to pursue higher education. Because of this, reading skills are prioritized in schools and society, and this can be good, particularly when considering the reading skills needed for college and career readiness as well as the impact that literacy skills have on social and economic opportunities.

As mentioned in our introduction, many adolescents do not yet read at grade level. In addition, adolescents need to learn new reading skills as they progress throughout middle and high school because they encounter or will encounter new kinds of written texts that require more sophisticated reading and writing skills and strategies. At the secondary level, reading assignments become longer, and across the subject areas, the texts students are asked to read tend to vary more. The intended audience, vocabulary, purpose, and text structure of texts in different subject areas also become more distinct. For example, history textbooks differ significantly from math and English Language Arts textbooks, not just in terms of content but also in how content is presented. As a result, some adolescents struggle with reading textbooks and other information-based documents across subject areas and subsequently struggle with writing tasks and assignments.

Academic reading and writing skills are indeed important to address at the secondary level, so throughout this book we will focus on these two literacy skills. A better understanding of these skills gives language and a framework for approaching other aspects of literacy. However, it's important to remember that literacy is much more than reading printed materials, which is where the "yes, and" component may be applied. Returning to our definition of literacy, humans acquire and use knowledge in particular contexts in various ways. Written texts are part of this, but so are aural (e.g., audiobooks, speeches, songs) and visual texts (e.g., movies, art, memes). As such, we readily acknowledge literacy needs to be broadly defined because it includes more than just reading.

With the dawn of the digital age and the increase of digital technologies and tools such as the Internet, Virtual Reality platforms, laptop computers, smartphones, and tablets, adolescents' access to different types of texts, particularly nonprint (e.g., websites, apps, videos, podcasts), has increased exponentially. In and out of school, today's adolescents are no longer solely reading and writing words in print-based texts. They're also reading, listening to, writing, watching, and creating texts on multiple digital devices and platforms (Hicks, 2021; Serafini & Gee, 2017; Hinchman & Appleman, 2017). Adolescents play video games, stream movies, watch YouTube videos and post their own content on social media channels. They listen to podcasts and playlists and read, comment on, and review websites. Literacy today needs to refer to reading and writing but also to all the ways we acquire, use, and produce knowledge in our 21st-century world.

Belief: Literacy Is a Generalized Skill

Many beginning teachers have heard the adage, "Learn to read by 3rd grade and then read to learn." This refers to the idea that once a student learns how to decode words, they can read anything. There's a similar understanding related to writing. Once a person learns to encode, they can write. Understanding reading and writing skills in this way makes sense because, indeed, certain fundamental skills are required in order to learn both. Additionally, there's truth in the fact that once we can read and write, technically we can and should be able to read and write anything. We might not understand everything we read, but we can almost always decode the words. One way that we like to help beginning teachers experience this phenomenon is by giving them a highly technical text about something they are unfamiliar with. They are almost always able to successfully decode the words in the text, but most of the time they don't fully understand what they've read.

This is where the "yes, and" idea comes into play. Literacy skills are generic and also specific. We might know how to decode words on a given page or screen, but depending on what those words are, how they are organized, and for what purpose, we might not understand them. This is because texts are written in different ways for different purposes and audiences. To successfully comprehend the texts we read, we must learn new words and concepts, connect old and new ideas, and understand how new texts are organized.

Although adolescents may be able to read and write (i.e., decode and encode) by the time they finish elementary school, the texts they routinely encounter in middle and high school are more complicated and specialized. They encounter new vocabulary, new text features and structures, new formats, and new styles. In a chemistry textbook, for example, complicated figures and charts display data. Primary source documents in a history class as well as Shakespeare's sonnets in an English Language Arts class include words and sentence structures unfamiliar to most adolescents. Calculus and algebraic equations differ significantly from elementary-level math equations. Similarly, scores of music are more complex and nuanced in secondary choir and band classes than in elementary music offerings. Moreover, the rules of engagement and types of games students learn in a secondary physical education class are more nuanced and complicated than those taught at the elementary level.

Although someone might be able to read effectively, if they don't have a working understanding of a particular subject matter, they may not understand what they read. Reading a treatise on quantum physics requires an understanding of both the genre (i.e., what a treatise is and its purpose) and the subject area itself. With this and other texts, it's possible to read the words in the text (i.e., decode) but have little to no idea about the content or meaning (i.e., comprehension). The same is true when students learn and engage in various writing genres. Although the language and conventions remain the same, genres differ. For instance, writing a short story requires a different set of skills and understanding than producing a commercial script, nutrition guide, poem, or lab report. In these instances, general writing skills (i.e., language and conventions) are similar, but the specifics (i.e., audience, purpose, tone, length, layout) are very different. Literacy skills are generic but also specific based on context.

Belief: Literary Development Is Finite

Connected to the understanding that literacy skills are generalizable, literacy development can be seen as linear and static. With this perspective, literacy is "achieved" when decoding, encoding, and fluency skills reach a certain level. This line of thinking suggests that adolescents' literacy skills are, or should be, fully developed by the time they enter middle and high school, especially if they were taught to read (i.e., decode) and write (i.e., encode) during their elementary years. It thus makes sense that literacy is many times seen as a one-and-done skill and not the responsibility of secondary teachers. When literacy is understood to be reading, and reading is thought of as the act of decoding words that should be learned by 3rd grade, it can be easy to assume that literacy is a linear process that can be learned and then applied. In fact, teacher education program requirements sometimes reinforce this assumption. Elementary teacher preparation and professional development focuses on early literacy instruction and formally teaching students how to read (i.e., decoding). Teacher education classes for secondary teachers, on the other hand, focus on disciplinary content and specific skills associated with a particular subject area.

Literacy development involves practice and skill development that occurs across a lifetime. While there are specific and discrete skills and knowledge that learners must learn, remember, and apply, literacy is more than a "one-and-done" skill. Rather than thinking about literacy as a one-time skill that is either mastered or not, a "yes, and" approach pushes us to consider literacy as a set of skills being continually developed. As adolescents' learning becomes more specialized within disciplines, adolescents must learn and apply new literacy skills to read, write, speak, view, listen, and represent in multiple subject areas and contexts, in and beyond school. They thus must continue to develop more nuanced and specialized literacy skills as they grow older.

Belief: Literacy Is School-Based

Another commonly held belief about literacy learning is that it happens only in school and can be effectively and fully measured on standardized assessments. Humans are naturally curious about how they compare to others. In a capitalistic society like the United States, ranking, scoring, and comparison are considered normal and generally expected. So, when we think about addressing and supporting adolescent literacy development, there is a push to conduct standardized and uniform ways to teach and assess learning (Gentry & Ouellette, 2019). Moreover, school-based literacy achievement is measured through standardized test scores (Elsesser, 2019; Sparks, 2022).

A "yes, and" approach helps us to recognize that these data fail to address all facets of adolescent literacy. Many skills and interests are not accounted for on standardized assessments. They don't showcase adolescents' entrepreneurial ideas and creative expressions. Standardized assessments aren't designed to capture how adolescents serve in, contribute to, and make differences in their communities and local economies. Even so, conversations about adolescent literacy tend to focus on the skills adolescents learn or demonstrate in school. These skills are important, but they represent only one context in which literacy skills occur; they center on academic-based literacy skills (i.e., skills needed to learn and demonstrate understanding of school subject matter).

As we consider how each of us acquires and uses specific knowledge in specific ways and contexts, we also need to consider different literacy experiences we have that involve hobbies, sports, religious practices, performing arts, popular culture, home, and work communities. Within each of these contexts, we use texts for different purposes, including social, political, and religious, and we create meanings from these varied texts in different ways. While adolescents might not be reading textbooks or assigned novels for an English Language Arts class, they are, in fact, actively decoding, comprehending, encountering new vocabulary, drawing on background knowledge, evaluating perspectives, and summarizing what they read on websites and social media as well as in magazines, manuals, and sacred texts such as the Bible and the Quran. These experiences, expertise, and the texts they encounter and use beyond school-based instructional contexts, however, are not always considered and valued because they aren't academic-focused and/or measurable.

Literacy researchers refer to these experiences and environments as "out-of-school" literacy practices (Hull & Schultz, 2002). These out-of-school practices aren't qualitatively different from what we learn in school, as many of the literacy practices and learning we do outside of school, in fact, overlap with what happens in school. As Donna Alvermann (Alvermann & Moore, 2011) posits, the different contexts in our lives act more as "sieves through which social, cultural, economic, and political discourses animate one another" (p. 158). In other words, what we do in the different contexts in our lives influences, informs, and motivates (or not) what we do in other contexts. What adolescents learn, know, and do outside school impacts what they learn, know, and do in school. We never "turn off" these other experiences, understandings, and expertise. While we might not be aware of or consciously draw on them, they influence us. Adolescents' out-of-school skills and experiences with reading and beyond can thus inform and support what happens in the classroom. For example, some adolescents write their own hip-hop or rap lyrics and create these for specific audiences and purposes. This could easily be acknowledged and affirmed during a poetry unit in an English Language Arts class.

Another important aspect of recognizing all contexts in which adolescents learn, develop, and use literacy skills is that adolescents who struggle with literacy in one context don't necessarily struggle in another. Adolescents might thrive in one subject area and struggle in another (Moje, 2002; NCTE, 2007). In addition, a math class might be hard for some adolescents at the same time as they are successfully running (and profiting from) a side business repairing small machines or working in retail.

School-based literacy represents a particular way of reading, writing, speaking, and listening and is accompanied by academic language (i.e., vocabulary associated with a given subject area). However, academic language isn't what most of us use in our everyday conversations. The way we write essays in history class or make claims and provide evidence in a debate class look and sound different from how we might write or argue in other contexts, such as persuading a parent to extend a weekend curfew or convincing an employer about a raise. Literacy is about the reading and writing that occurs in school but also describes what we do in other contexts.

Belief: Literacy Instruction Is the Responsibility of English Language Arts Teachers

At the secondary level, adolescent literacy instruction is often assumed to be the responsibility of English Language Arts teachers, seen by other teachers as being "the" reading and writing teachers. After all, the curriculum in English Language Arts classes centers on reading and writing, in contrast to other subject areas such as math, music, art, physical education and health, science, and social studies. Although these subjects also include reading and writing, they are viewed as a means to an end rather than a perceived end, as many believe reading and writing are in English Language Arts classes.

Additionally, most secondary teachers enter the profession with a passion for their chosen discipline or subject area. At the secondary level, the subject is foregrounded, and subject-specific courses make up the majority of teacher education preparation at the secondary level. Many times it is understood that a secondary teacher's job is to teach the subject matter (e.g., a history teacher teaches history; a physical education teacher teaches physical education, and sometimes health). This being the case, being told that literacy instruction needs to be part of every secondary teacher's job can feel like an "add on" to the already difficult and complicated task of teaching a subject matter to adolescents. Some teachers might feel that devoting time to reading or writing instruction makes it more challenging to cover subject matter important to their course.

A "yes, and" approach, however, maintains that literacy support is integral to subject matter knowledge. We encourage beginning teachers to see adolescent literacy instruction as a way to pay attention to how they introduce, explain, and support adolescents as they acquire, use, and produce knowledge in their subject area. Paying attention to this is even more important in the middle and high school years because of how significantly subject matter changes with more specialized and different kinds of texts used and knowledge acquired. Subjects become increasingly different from one another as grade levels rise, and attention to these differences is vital.

Generic literacy skills and strategies can be taught and encouraged across all subject areas. Still, increasingly specialized literacy skills within each discipline must also be addressed, as we will explore in later chapters. In English Language Arts, for example, the particular ways of reading and writing differ significantly from the reading and writing tasks and skills that occur in other subject areas.

It's important to acknowledge that secondary teachers are not reading specialists or literacy coaches, roles sometimes used interchangeably and other times defined uniquely. Reading specialists are teachers with specialized training in teaching reading who, more than not, work in elementary schools. They help determine which students need more support with reading by administering reading assessments and working directly with students in small groups or one on one to provide support and instruction. Literacy coaches are former teachers with specialized and advanced training in literacy instruction and support. They generally work with teachers to improve their skills in literacy instruction, focusing on supporting teachers' reading and writing instruction. The responsibilities of reading specialists and literacy coaches tend to differ depending on the school and/or district. While not every school district has these positions, it's important for secondary teachers who do have access to reading specialists and literacy coaches to work alongside them and to use them as important resources in the work of supporting all adolescents' literacy development. Special education teachers and English as a Second Language (ESL) teachers can also be important resources and collaborators. Their expertise in reading disabilities and language acquisition can serve all secondary teachers as they support adolescent learners' literacy development.

Belief: Literacy Instruction Is One Size Fits All

Literacy development needs to occur across subject areas and in consistent ways because adolescent learners benefit from hearing similar language and processes across the different classes they take. One class or teacher alone cannot sufficiently support adolescents' literacy development; literacy instruction must be supported by teachers across subject areas as well as by administrators. Thus there are many schoolwide literacy initiatives, curricula, and programs to support literacy instruction across the subject areas.

Schoolwide literacy efforts result in many benefits, and we are glad for the ways they bring attention to literacy development and provide much-needed resources to support teachers' own literacy learning and pedagogical efforts. A "yes, and" approach to these initiatives is to recognize that literacy instruction is more complex than what any one-size-fits-all method, strategy, or approach can provide. So, while these schoolwide efforts can be successful, recognition that there isn't one "perfect" curriculum, teaching method, or text to ensure that all learners will be equally successful is also needed. In a competitive market of instruction and curricular materials, companies market easy solutions and hard-to-keep promises in their efforts to sell their programs to school decision-makers. It is thus important for teachers to understand what informs the instructional materials and interventions they use.

For example, some materials are research based, which are practices or interventions rigorously tested and found to be effective through research. Research-based means they have been subjected to scientific scrutiny and shown to produce positive results. Other literacy curriculum and interventions aimed to support adolescents' learning are research informed, which means they have been developed with the input of research but may not have been rigorously tested. Research-informed materials and strategies may be based on the findings of research but may not have been subjected to the same level of scrutiny as research-based practices.

In general, research-based practices are more reliable and effective than research-informed practices. However, research-informed practices can still be valuable, especially if there is limited research available on a particular topic. Also, note that "research-based" and "research-informed" are not mutually exclusive. A practice or intervention can be both. This means that it has been rigorously tested and found to be effective, and it has also been developed with the input of research. While both rely on research in different ways, no one curriculum or literacy-based intervention has been found to work for every student in every context (Dilgard & Hodges, 2022).

An unintended consequence of assuming that a specific curriculum or literacy intervention will work for everyone is evidenced when the underachievement of certain groups of students is framed as a "technical" problem that calls for specific, one-size-fits-all solutions such as using the "right" teaching methods, strategies, or prepackaged curricula. For instance, adolescents who come to school not yet ready to learn can be viewed as having linguistic and/or cognitive deficits, separate from adolescents who have diagnosed learning needs and challenges. Such deficits, often determined by standardized test scores or students' previous academic performance, may be attributed to poor or ineffective parenting, socioeconomic status, and/or limited linguistic models in their homes and communities (Emdin, 2016). This means that teachers must utilize a "yes, and" approach when it comes to evaluating, selecting, curating, and implementing curriculum materials and interventions. In doing so, teachers consider multiple sources of information about adolescents' needs and contexts, including academic records and performance as well as students' contexts, interests, and needs. When they do so, teachers will better understand how to select and use curricular resources, materials, and interventions in ways that effectively support their adolescents' needs.

We've also seen this oversimplification occur in many literacy-related professional development experiences at the secondary level. For example, teachers from across subject areas attend a workshop led by an outside "literacy expert" who tries to convince them to use the same three reading strategies in all their classes, no matter the grade level or subject matter, with the assurance that all students will benefit. While this may be the case, a "yes, and" approach clarifies that at the secondary level the texts and subject matter are more specialized, which requires general strategies but also discipline-specific approaches.

In some instances, increasing the number of literacy-focused strategies without scaffolded and purposeful instruction and/or clarity about why the strategy is specifically useful decreases student engagement and motivation for learning. Expecting all teachers to use the same strategies and approaches with different students, in different contexts, and in different subject areas at the secondary level does not actually result in students' uniform literacy growth and achievement. Focusing on implementing one-size-fits-all strategies can sometimes lead to implementing strategies that are not well suited to a teacher's instruction or a particular subject area, as noted earlier.

A strategy that works well in a freshmen-level physical education or math class will not necessarily work well in a 9th-grade band class (Conley, 2008). While many strategies can be used in more than one subject area, the unique literacy demands of each discipline require that these strategies be embedded and discussed in the work of each discipline in authentic ways. For example, a close reading approach should be framed and applied differently in an English Language Arts class than in an art or music class, where language and corresponding symbols are used differently and for different purposes. Increases in reading and writing tasks may be valid and useful, but the payoff will be limited if they aren't purposeful or aligned with disciplinary practices (Fisher et al., 2016).

Furthermore, adolescents aren't all the same and have different literacy needs. With literacy instruction, it's equally important to consider the specific literacy needs of different students in various contexts (Dresser, 2012). Using a particular literacy strategy as part of a schoolwide literacy effort might not work without the necessary and sometimes discipline-specific instruction and scaffolding to increase adolescents' stamina and support their understanding and motivation.

SECONDARY SCHOOL READING INITIATIVES

In some schools, teachers of all subject areas are asked to have students read independently for a certain number of minutes each week or to increase the number of written assignments given to students based on the claims that these changes will lead to a dramatic increase in students' reading and writing scores. In fact, a beginning teacher one of us worked with explained a new writing initiative in their school. Instead of challenging teachers to increase the writing instruction and writing specific to each subject area, teachers were told that every student in every class needed to write more essays, intended to help students perform well on an upcoming national standardized assessment.

Many of the subject-area teachers balked at this because essay writing didn't fit or align with the specific writing skills and genres associated with their subject matter. In this instance, writing more essays in a music, art, or math class would not necessarily serve students' literacy development in those areas. While reading independently and writing are important initiatives, such approaches do not always accomplish the intended goal of further developing adolescents' literacy skills and knowledge.

Belief: Literacy Instruction Is Skills Based

When we consider how to support adolescents' literacy development, it can be easy to assume that the way to do so is to focus on literacy skills and help not-yet-proficient readers acquire decoding and encoding skills. Approached in this way, literacy instruction can be seen as needing to focus on skills and skills alone. In fact, most of the examples shared so far focus on supporting adolescent students' reading and writing skill development.

Skill instruction and explicit instruction around literacy strategies are important and have been proven successful in supporting adolescent literacy development. For adolescent students diagnosed with reading and/or writing disabilities, skill instruction can be an important part of the support they need. However, a "yes, and" approach helps us understand that adolescent literacy instruction needs to involve more than skill development.

While skills are part of literacy development, our skill development is also connected with motivation and engagement. Literacy is also social and embedded within different communities. Our identities are central to the kinds of reading, writing, speaking, listening, and viewing activities in which we engage, and this contributes to who we are and how we want to be seen in the world. Skills must thus be embedded with identity, motivation, and engagement. Students need and want to know what they're learning and why. Their learning also needs to be relevant to their interests, experiences, and lives. Reading comprehension research has proven that motivation and engagement must be considered when supporting students' comprehension of texts (Fisher et al., 2016).

Thus, when we think about adolescent literacy instruction and support, we need to include more than just school-based skills and strategies. Particularly when considering adolescence as a unique age and stage of life, the concept of motivation needs to be addressed. Many adolescent students who are not yet proficient try to hide their lagging skills. Others have been in ineffective reading intervention programs for years, working with leveled reading texts that are not interesting or relevant. During adolescence, teens have a strong desire for acceptance, belonging, admiration, and respect. When we add feelings of anxiety, shame, and frustration that can occur around school literacy tasks, particularly for struggling readers, skills cannot be the sole focus of literacy instruction. As we've seen in our own classrooms and with the teachers with whom we work, adolescents need support to develop confidence, find motivation, and acquire skills for the specialized academic literacies in their middle and high school courses, and this can be done in so many creative and subject-focused ways.

MOVING FORWARD

In the following chapters, we explore various understandings of literacy, adolescent literacy, and adolescent literacy instruction, including how these understandings serve to inform secondary teachers' work with adolescents and how a "yes, and" approach enhances teachers' understanding and affords additional ways to enhance pedagogy and practice that directly benefit the adolescents in their classrooms. As already noted, adolescent literacy centers on how learners, ages 10 to 18, acquire and use specific knowledge for specific purposes in a given context. Using this definition, adolescent literacy entails much more than reading and involves general and specific skills. Adolescent literacy instruction, a responsibility of all teachers, is multifaceted and needs to address skill development but also adolescents' motivation for learning and the unique disciplinary demands associated with each subject area.

Questions to Consider

- *Which of the commonly held beliefs discussed in the chapter do (or did) you hold?*
- *Which "yes, and" statements resonate most with you?*
- *How might you use adolescents' expertise to support their literacy development in your subject area(s)?*

CHAPTER 2

Adolescents' Literacy Skills

KEY TERMS

Background knowledge: the information, experiences, and skills across contexts that a person acquires throughout their lifetime that provides a basis for understanding a topic or subject
Comprehension: the state of having understood something
Fluency: the ability to express oneself clearly in a given language
Vocabulary: the words that make up a particular language or subject area—may also refer to all the known words used by a particular person

Building on what we know about adolescents, adolescence, and commonly held beliefs about literacy, it's important for secondary teachers to understand adolescents' literacy skills, including the fundamental skills involved in learning to read and write. In this chapter, we focus on three "yes, and" approaches to commonly held beliefs about literacy, including that literacy is both general and specific skills; literacy development is ongoing; and literacy instruction is the responsibility of all teachers.

Knowing the skills involved in reading and writing gives teachers important insights into why adolescent students might find particular content and literacy tasks challenging.

When we consider the literacy skills adolescents require to be successful, it's important to consider multiple aspects of students' literacy development and both collective and individual needs. In our conversations with beginning teachers, it's important to explore the following questions related to why adolescent students might be struggling in class:

- Is it that they don't know the meaning of some words?
- Are they not yet able to effectively monitor their comprehension?
- Are they making connections between ideas in the text?
- Are they not yet able to make inferences?
- Might they struggle coming up with the right words to express an idea or concept (in writing or verbally)?
- Have they not yet developed fluency with particular writing skills?

- Is it possible they feel overwhelmed by a reading and/or writing assignment?
- Is their confidence or motivation impacting their ability to fully engage with reading and/or writing tasks?
- Is it a combination of things, or maybe something else entirely?

When teachers can identify and understand their students' needs, they can better support students' literacy development. The approaches teachers may take to address these particular needs, however, vary.

THREE APPROACHES TO LITERACY INSTRUCTION

Though secondary teachers may not be directly impacted by different approaches to and debates about early literacy instruction, it's important for secondary teachers to have a general understanding of them. These approaches can inform instruction at the secondary level, given that adolescents' literacy development is ongoing and secondary teachers play an important role in that development, not only in support of students' general literacy skills but also those specific to a given subject area (e.g., learning to read, write, play music in band and orchestra classes). Additionally, a general understanding of different approaches to early literacy instruction can inform secondary teachers' work with students who may not yet be proficient in particular areas and/or who may benefit from specific supports and approaches.

In the paragraphs below, we offer a basic overview of three approaches to early literacy instruction. Our purpose is not to provide a comprehensive account of each but rather to orient beginning teachers to conversations around literacy instruction so they are better able to identify differing literacy theories, approaches, and practices.

Science of Reading Approach

A science of reading approach refers to a body of research rooted in cognitive scientists' work related to how humans learn to read. One of the most frequently referenced books focused on a science of reading approach is Dehaene's (2009) book *Reading in the Brain: The New Science of How We Read*. Dehaene writes: "The goal of reading instruction is clear. It must aim to lay down an efficient neuronal hierarchy so that the child can recognize letters and graphemes and easily turn them into speech sounds" (p. 118). This approach to reading instruction focuses on specific, hierarchical steps and stages in the teaching of reading and is sometimes referred to as a "bottom-up" approach (Pearson, 2004).

In many ways, a science of reading approach is about teaching learners the specific mental "moves" involved in being able to read. When learning English, one example of a "move" is the use of phonics instruction to teach children how to read. Using phonics instruction, educators teach students to associate letters or groups of letters with the sounds they make, and to use this knowledge to decode words. In a science of reading approach, phonics instruction is typically taught systematically, starting with the simplest letter–sound relationships and progressing to more complex ones. Children are taught to blend sounds together to form words, and to break words down into their individual sounds. This helps them to decode unfamiliar words and develop the skills they need to become fluent readers.

The science of reading approach has many strong advocates and continues to gain traction in elementary curricula and instruction as well as policy initiatives at the state and national levels. This emphasis on skills, particularly for early learners, has led to many debates centered on how and why to teach these skills. However, various definitions abound for what this approach refers to, so much so that some scholars have started to differentiate between popular media definitions of the science of reading and research-based definitions (Aukerman, 2022). Descriptions of this approach in popular media tend to focus solely on phonics instruction. Note that while this approach does emphasize a systematic, highly structured approach to teaching phonics, it also emphasizes other domains, such as comprehension (Duke et al., 2021; Hoffman et al., 2021; Wyse & Bradbury, 2022). At the elementary level, other components include teaching vocabulary and providing opportunities for children to practice their reading skills through independent reading and guided reading activities.

Whole-Language Approach

Described by Pressley et al. (2023) as a "meaning emphasis" approach, whole-literacy instruction focuses on the natural competence of literacy development through immersion in real literature and daily writing activities. In contrast to a bottom-up skill development approach, a whole-language approach is top down (Pearson, 2004) with its holistic view of reading and foregrounding of meaning and context (Goodman, 1986, 1989).

Whole-language proponents argue that children should be taught to read by reading authentic texts and books, not by being drilled in phonics and other isolated skills. They believe that children learn to read by using language in meaningful contexts, such as reading and writing stories, songs, and poems. Whole-language proponents also believe that children should be encouraged to use their own background knowledge and experiences to make sense of what they read and write. Reading instruction, within a whole-language approach, focuses on exposing students to good books and spending instructional time on the ideas and stories within these books.

The whole-language instructional model has been criticized for its lack of emphasis on phonics and other basic skills. Critics argue that children taught using the whole-language approach are more likely to struggle with reading comprehension and fluency. However, proponents of whole language have argued that their approach is more effective in the long run, as it helps children develop a love of reading and a strong foundation in language skills.

Balanced Literacy Approach

The term "balanced literacy" was popularized in the mid-1990s with the intention of drawing on the best elements of both previously described approaches by emphasizing "immersion in authentic literacy-related experiences and extensive explicit teaching through modeling, explanation and mini lesson re-explanations, especially with respect to decoding and other skills" (Wharton-McDonald et al., 1998 p. 518). With a balanced literacy approach, teachers use both teacher-led reading and writing instruction and independent reading to teach phonics, vocabulary, fluency, and comprehension and also to encourage students to read and write for a variety of purposes, such as for pleasure, for information, and for self-expression (Calkins, 1986, Fountas & Pinnell, 2007).

Over the years, balanced literacy's "middle ground" has come to refer to a wide variety of choices related to text selection, text types, instruction, groupings, skills, and strategies (Fisher et al., 2023). Critics argue that unless paired with specific skill instruction and development, applying a balanced literacy approach doesn't benefit not-yet-proficient readers nearly as much as it does those who are already proficient (Winter, 2022).

Making Sense of Differing Approaches

The brief overview of these approaches illustrates the complex landscape of literacy instruction. Each approach represents a different literacy theory, approach, and practice, and within each are differing purposes, outcomes, and underlying assertions. When encountering new literacy initiatives, policies, curricula, and professional development opportunities, it can be helpful to understand which approach they might be coming from and why, as well as the associated criticisms.

In the rest of this chapter we will unpack terms and concepts associated with these approaches by providing language and a framework for learning about, noticing, and supporting students' reading and writing skills.

READING AND WRITING SKILLS

Within this larger context of literacy instruction, we focus primarily on reading and writing skills in this chapter, although literacy skills also include speaking, listening, viewing, and representing. The dominance of reading and writing skills and their importance in school contexts warrants that teachers have a clear understanding of what it means to read and write. Reading and writing processes and effective instructional approaches have been well researched and documented, and this knowledge provides an excellent foundation and springboard for understanding the literacy skills adolescents also need for speaking, listening, viewing, visually representing, and performing. Though verbal, aural, and visual skills are different from reading and writing skills, some common language can be used across all modes of literacy when thinking about skill development. This knowledge empowers teachers to identify, respond to, and support adolescents' literacy learning needs.

Learning to Read

When people talk about the fundamentals of learning to read, they refer to what happens or needs to happen in humans' brains as we make sense of words on a page. These are called cognitive processes. Studying these processes, theorists and researchers closely examine what's happening inside a learner's brain and body to understand how humans acquire specific literacy skills and how they learn. For example, in the field of cognitive psychology, researchers have studied and tracked the human brain as it performs various tasks and behaviors related to reading. They do this to understand what happens when reading occurs and to build "living maps of the neuronal landscape" (Willingham, 2015, p. 21).

As a result, researchers study what needs to happen in our brains before and when we learn to read words, sentences, and paragraphs. Gentry and Ouellette (2019) note that "we now know that reading is a complex cognitive process; it involves many complicated processing systems [inside the brain] that must act in concert. Reading activates areas of the brain from the back, posterior regions through to the frontal lobe, and many areas in between" (p. 15). These complex cognitive processes include learning to consider what our eyes see on a page, such as letters, words, phrases, and sentences, translating them into ideas in our minds, and then turning these ideas into coherent thoughts. Being able to read means these complex cognitive processes have become automatic to us.

Despite debates over how to teach our brains to do these processes, the consensus is that the reading process is not as natural as speaking and that most children benefit from explicit instruction in decoding. As Seidenberg

(2017) argues, "cultural, economic and educational circumstances obviously affect children's progress [in learning to read] . . . but what they need to learn does not change" (p. 101). Over the years, researchers have championed the idea of a clear and linear progression through these stages and that the reading process is supported in specific ways (Willingham, 2015; Wolf, 2008).

Stages of Learning to Read

Earlier researchers concluded that this process of learning to read occurs in distinct and linear developmental stages (Chall, 1983; Ehri, 1999). The first four stages are associated with childhood, and the additional two connect with adolescence and adulthood. Discussions and debates persist over some of the details of these different stages, but the consensus is that these stages progress one after the other in a predictable, linear fashion.

- **The prereading stage**, otherwise known as stage 0, starts when a child is very young and begins to accumulate knowledge about the nature and structure of letters, words, and books.
- **The decoding stage** occurs next when children learn how to put sounds and letters together into words and start to recognize spelling patterns. This stage occurs in early elementary school.
- **Confirmation or fluency** exists when a child's knowledge about letters and words is put into practice with the ability to read what is known or familiar. In this stage, children gain courage and skill and grow in fluency and reading speed.
- **Reading for learning the new** is the next stage, in which children use their reading ability to gain new knowledge and information. In this stage, children read straightforward texts that present one viewpoint. The adage "learn to read and then read to learn" refers to arriving at this "reading for learning new" stage.
- **Multiple viewpoints** occurs in adolescence and is the stage at which readers can read and make sense of texts that include multiple viewpoints.
- **Construction and reconstruction** refers to when readers read for one's purposes, selectively using what they read to advance their knowledge and interests; this stage occurs in late adolescence and adulthood.

Five Pillars of Literacy

In our conversations with beginning teachers, we refer to findings from the National Reading Panel's (2000) report on comprehension strategy instruction. The authors of this report reviewed roughly 100,000 reading studies and identified five key concepts at the core of effective reading instruction programs. These concepts, in no hierarchical order, include phonemic awareness, phonics, fluency, vocabulary, and comprehension. The report is not focused on the stages of learning to read or on how reading skills are most effectively taught (i.e., which instructional methods, approaches, and materials are most beneficial). Although more than 20 years old now, this report continues to be referenced and used in the literacy field to inform literacy instruction (Shanahan, 2005; Cassidy et al., 2010; Cassidy et al., 2020).

We use these five pillars to start conversations with secondary teachers about reading skills and instruction. Most secondary teachers we work with have little or no familiarity with the process of learning to read, aside from their own experiences doing so. The pillars help beginning teachers identify what adolescent readers might be struggling with, or conversely what skills adolescents might have already mastered. Further, the five pillars can help beginning teachers explain and even normalize to adolescents why they might be struggling with the complex texts they encounter in different subject areas. It can be easy to assume that some English Learners, for example, are not able to read when in reality they know how to decode words and might have extensive vocabularies in their home and/or first language(s). As we discuss later, reading also includes important components such as knowledge and motivation, which are particularly important to consider when supporting adolescents' literacy development.

Pillar 1: Phonemic Awareness

Phonemic awareness refers to the ability to hear, understand, and use the sounds that word parts make. Phonemes are the smallest units of sound that distinguish words from each other. Since sounds can't be written, in English we use letters to represent the different sounds. Phonemes, which can include consonant or vowel sounds, are joined together to form words. The English language is complex and has approximately 44 phonemes, represented by each letter of the English alphabet and by combinations of letters. In addition, hundreds of spelling alternatives can be used to represent these 44 English phonemes. The sound of "g" as in "grapes" is also made with these "g" letter variations: "gg," "gh," "gu," and "gue" (e.g., egg, ghost, guest, league). The word "cat" (i.e., c-a-t) is made up of three letters and three sounds (i.e., /kat/), just as the word "shook" (i.e., s-h-o-o-k) is also made up of three sounds (i.e., /SHook/), although it has five letters.

Phonemic awareness also refers to identifying and using individual sound units in different combinations. Phonemes can be added together (e.g., sick to slick), blended (e.g., s-at), deleted (e.g., frog to fog), segmented (e.g., k-at = cat), and substituted (e.g., sled to sped). For example, taking the word "dish" and changing the first phoneme to a different one to make the word "fish." Or, finding rhyming words with a particular word. "Tab," for example, rhymes with "cab," "lab," "glad," "mad," "sad." Phonemic awareness is a skill that can be generalized to many different contexts, and typically once it is learned, this skill has been mastered. Students who have dyslexia, a learning disorder and reading disability, can struggle with phonemic awareness because of individual differences in the areas of their brains that process language.

Pillar 2: Phonics

Phonics is understanding a predictable relationship between phonemes (sounds) and graphemes (i.e., letters representing those sounds). For example, it is learning that the word "star" is made up of four distinct sounds but has only one syllable, and is thus pronounced "star." Phonics gives students a rule-based system for reading that can help them recognize familiar words, decode new words, and pronounce unknown words. Phonics instruction thus teaches students the relationships between letters or letter combinations, sounds, and syllables and how to use those relationships to build words. Phonics also teaches students a way to remember how to read words so they can read, spell, and recognize words. For example, students learn that "ch" and "sh" make particular sounds. As students memorize these sound symbols, they learn the code of reading. In fact, the term "cracking the code" of reading refers to when someone can use phonics to start decoding words. Phonics builds on the skill of phonemic awareness and represents another skill that can be learned no matter the context or text.

Pillar 3: Fluency

Fluency is the ability to read text accurately, expressively, and quickly to oneself or aloud. It's the ability to read as we speak and verbalize our understanding of texts. For example, television, movie, and stage actors must be fluent when delivering their lines during a performance. When readers no longer struggle with decoding words, they are freed up to focus their attention on the meaning of a text. This comes as the result of being able to read in phrases instead of carefully sounding out individual words. It also involves being able to read with pitch, tone, volume, and pauses. Fluent readers will pause briefly when they see a comma used in a sentence. And they will pause a bit longer at a period signaling the end of a sentence. When reading dialogue or sentences describing emotion, they will add expression and/or vary their tone. If they see bold or italicized words in a text, they know to emphasize these words. Unlike phonemic awareness and phonics, fluency represents a different kind of skill, as it can depend on what is being read. Readers may have phonemic awareness and an understanding of phonics, but if a text contains too many unknown words or relies on too much background information that readers do not have, fluency might not occur.

For many secondary teachers, the first three pillars are not explicitly taught or addressed at the secondary level, unless there is explicit language instruction or special education support provided. However, it is important for secondary teachers to understand the literacy development processes adolescents are expected to have already experienced prior to entering middle and high school classrooms. This provides helpful contextual and background knowledge, as secondary teachers most often focus their instruction and attention on the fourth and fifth pillars (vocabulary and comprehension). These are particularly important aspects of adolescents' literacy development, and secondary teachers need to actively support and develop both. In addition to the overviews of both pillars below, we explore how to support adolescents' vocabulary development and comprehension in more detail in Chapter 5.

Pillar 4: Vocabulary

Vocabulary refers to reading and understanding words, both orally and in print. Most vocabulary is learned indirectly through our everyday reading, writing, speaking, and listening experiences, both in and out of school. Many scholars estimate that students enter kindergarten knowing 5,000 to 10,000 words—though as we describe below, this can vary widely—and graduate high school with a vocabulary of 50,000 words (Nagy & Herman, 1987; Graves & Sales, 2008). Vocabulary matters because research shows a relationship between the size of a students' vocabulary and their reading comprehension level. This relationship becomes more significant as students progress through school (Snow et al., 2007; Swanson et al., 2017).

The term "vocabulary gap" refers to the differences between the number of words different groups of students are exposed to and/or have obtained. A family's socioeconomic status and parental education can contribute to students' vocabulary sizes. According to Sperry et al. (2019), debates persist among scholars over how wide this vocabulary gap is and what contributes to it. That said, the consensus remains that some students have larger vocabularies than others, and this affects their school achievement, particularly because of the sizable academic vocabulary needed at the secondary level to understand concepts, objects, and processes in several subject areas. Students who have larger vocabularies understand more of what they read and, thus, when they encounter new and more complex texts continue to increase their vocabularies, as well as their content knowledge. If students have a limited vocabulary, which is true for English

Learners and students who have had limited exposure to and engagement with varied texts, the opposite often occurs.

Teachers in all subject areas expect adolescents to know and be able to define and use vocabulary connected to their learning (Beck et al., 2013). With increasingly complex texts across the subject areas, adolescent students will encounter words they don't know. One aspect of vocabulary instruction should center on students learning word prefixes, suffixes, and roots to support their vocabulary acquisition, with the intention that students will learn what these mean and, in doing so, expand their vocabulary knowledge. Knowing the patterns and systems for words can empower students when they encounter words they don't know or remember. For example, in English, when students learn that the prefix "pre" means "before," they are more likely to know or make an educated guess as to the meanings of other words that start with this prefix (e.g., predict, prevent, prenatal, pre-read). Thus, effective vocabulary instruction centers on teaching students specific, concrete patterns and rules they can apply to new words they encounter in the texts they read, listen to, and/or watch.

Teachers can also teach students word analysis strategies that can help them decode multisyllabic words. For example, teachers can look for multisyllabic, high-frequency, specialized, and nonspecialized academic words in their subject area(s) and then determine which words students may struggle with. "Flagellants," "bubonic," and "dissolution" in a history text are specific words that may need to be explicitly taught or analyzed, whereas the terms, "onomatopoeia," "alliteration," and "denouement" would more likely be addressed and taught in an English Language Arts class. Every subject area has specialized vocabulary students need to know, understand, and use. This means secondary teachers must integrate vocabulary instruction when and where it is needed to support adolescents' literacy development in their specific subject areas.

Vocabulary challenges also arise when the same word, in two different contexts, means two different things. At the secondary level, the meanings of many words vary from context to context and subject area to subject area. For example, in the English language, when someone talks about the game-changing interception in last week's football game, it is important to know that they are not talking about last night's precipitation that was intercepted by leaves, something a geologist might discuss when reflecting on a late afternoon rainstorm. The word "intercept" is used in both instances (i.e., football and precipitation), but based on context the word has far different meanings.

Many secondary teachers focus their instruction on helping adolescents identify and define subject-specific words and terms, testing students' vocabulary knowledge separate from any application of the terms. For example, at the beginning of a new unit, a teacher may send students home with lists of terms they expect students to look up and write definitions for. These definition lists are then turned in as part of the students' homework. Although students could identify the words and definitions, either through online or app-based dictionary resources, it would never really be clear if the students fully understood the meanings of the vocabulary words or how to use them in the context of what they were learning in their biology class, for example. In this instance, vocabulary would have been assigned, but not explicitly taught; unfortunately, this means that these words may or may not have been added to students' overall vocabulary.

Pillar 5: Comprehension

Reading comprehension refers to attaining meaning from what we read and, simply put, is the reason that we read. According to the authors of the RAND Reading Study Group (2002), comprehension is "the process of simultaneously extracting and constructing meaning through interaction and involvement with written language" (p. 11). Some researchers describe reading comprehension as the result of decoding skills (i.e., phonemic awareness, phonics, and fluency) combined with language comprehension (i.e., vocabulary knowledge and the ability to create meaning from words in a sentence). This understanding of reading comprehension is known as a "simple view of reading" (Gough & Tunmer, 1986), associated with a science of reading approach.

Other scholars suggest that additional factors also contribute to one's ability to comprehend what is read. This view, described as a "complex view of reading" (Duke & Cartwright, 2021; Kim, 2017), is an approach to understanding the reading process that recognizes that reading, including comprehension, is a multifaceted and complex skill involving the interaction of various cognitive processes. This view recognizes that reading is not simply the process of decoding printed words but also involves the reader's background knowledge, word-reading skill, vocabulary knowledge, inference making, reading comprehension, and reading strategies used when accessing various texts (Cervetti et al., 2020).

Background Knowledge

While background knowledge isn't identified as one of the five pillars, secondary teachers need to pay extra attention to the importance it plays in contributing to adolescents' reading comprehension. In our work with beginning teachers, we use the term "background knowledge" to refer to everything a learner knows about an idea or topic within a text and how this knowledge must get activated for new knowledge to be added. Some scholars differentiate between "background" and "prior" knowledge, distinguishing between specific knowledge that helps students clarify and better understand new material and more general knowledge from personal, cultural, and educational experiences that helps students connect new material to already known concepts and ideas. For simplicity's sake, we use "background knowledge" to refer to all of the general and specific knowledge that students already have. If we read the word "doctor," for example, our previous experiences with or different understandings of who doctors are and what they do will be activated. For some, their background knowledge of "doctor" might include a lab coat and a person working in a hospital. Others might draw on their knowledge of academics who receive a graduate degree, such as a PhD, and still others might think of their family physician or people who work in their local health center, dentist office, or optometry shop.

Connected to vocabulary and comprehension, background knowledge is important because it offers mental building blocks upon which readers can rely as they read and learn. When learning something new through reading, learners' brains are wired to connect one unit to another, using background knowledge as a base upon which to build. Learners' ability to comprehend what they read, listen to, or watch is thus directly tied to their ability to assimilate textual information into existing schemata or change their schema as they incorporate new information (An, 2013).

When learning about biomes in biology class, for example, students are expected to connect this concept to other concepts they already have in their memories about plants and animals (including what animals eat and where they live). They are also taught to associate biomes with vegetation types, such as coniferous forests and grasslands. So, if a 6th-grade science teacher introduces the concept of a biome and uses an article or textbook segment as part of their instruction, this teacher would count on students connecting what they already know (i.e., their schema) with what they learn from the assigned text. As students read, they are expected to connect their background knowledge of animals, including what animals need to survive, with what they learn about biomes (i.e., flora and fauna within major habitats). When making these connections while they read, the schemata students have related to their understanding of ecology and biology increases.

As Patterson et al. (2018) argue, adding to a learner's background knowledge is critical for supporting students' learning in the sciences. In fact, building learners' background knowledge, where they connect what they read and learn to what they already know, is critical for supporting learning in all subject areas (An, 2013). Thus, a secondary teacher's role is to help their students connect their background knowledge with new knowledge.

Learning to Write

In addition to understanding what is involved in learning to read, beginning teachers must also have a deeper understanding of writing skills and development. Cognitive understandings of how humans learn to write have influenced the research on writing, but much of the writing instruction research has occurred in fields outside of psychology, including composition, rhetoric, and literature. Scholars argue that writing development, like reading, occurs in predictable, sequential phases and that, also like reading, writing is not a natural process (Liberman et al., 1989). Part of this writing development process involves learning to encode. Encoding refers to the ability to use letter and sound knowledge to write. In other words, a writer needs to draw on phonemic awareness and phonics skills to pull sounds apart in words, match letters to sounds, and then inscribe those letters on paper or in type. In this way, reading and spelling are paired because to do one well, you need to do the other.

Stages of Learning to Write

Some researchers have identified stages of learning to write that focus on spelling and encoding words. Bear et al. (2016), for example, identify four stages of writing: emergent, beginning, transitional, and intermediate and specialized.

- **Emergent** (ages 1–7) is the stage consisting of pretend writing or drawing.
- **Beginning** (ages 5–9) focuses on writing each syllable of a word, writing summaries, and/or retelling stories.
- **Transitional** (ages 6–12) is when writers become more fluent in writing and spend more time planning their writing; at this stage, writing is more organized and includes more details.
- **Intermediate and Specialized Writing** (ages 10–100) is the stage at which writers are considered fluent and can independently understand and effectively write different genres and styles, including accurate use of tone and expression.

While debate persists over more or fewer stages of learning to write (Kress, 2016), it is generally accepted that the stages are organized in a linear sequence and that one stage must be completed before the next one can begin. Some researchers have pushed on this theory and proposed that learning to write involves not linear stages but mental processes that have a hierarchical structure (Flower & Hayes, 1981). What all these writing theories have in common is that they point to how writing skills must be developed over time, can be supported in particular ways, and require abundant practice.

Writing Instruction

Identifying students' writing needs and supporting them as they develop their writing skills and proficiency is important work within each subject area. When adolescents are not-yet-proficient writers, they may feel challenged by one or more aspects of writing development. They might struggle as they move from one subject area to another, trying to make sense of the various genres, writing styles, audiences, and purposes within each. They might struggle with dyslexia or dysgraphia. Others may not yet have developed the fluency or automaticity with particular writing skills, so writing might feel overwhelming, laborious, or frustrating. Some students may not be proficient in coming up with the right words to express an idea or concept. Still others might not yet be proficient in their abilities to develop their thoughts fluently and clearly. Some might experience a hard time getting started with a writing assignment and feel overwhelmed. Further, some adolescents might have writing proficiency but are not confident in their writing, which may contribute to a lack of motivation for some assignments.

Supporting students' writing development is generally framed in terms of two goals: learning to write (i.e., learning the skills to encode words) and writing to learn (i.e., using writing to learn content). The skills involved in learning to write are categorized into two sets of skills: transcription skills such as punctuation, capitalization, spelling, handwriting/keyboarding; and composing skills that employ the writing process such as prewriting, planning, drafting, and revision (Sedita, 2013).

By adolescence, students need to develop writing skills so they can express meaning in written forms in ways that come automatically to them. Being "fluent" in writing occurs when learners apply the rules of spelling, handwriting/keyboarding skills, and grammar to communicate clearly and effectively. Sometimes these skills are referred to as the mechanics of writing or as grammar. At times, adolescent learners might need additional support with the physical components of writing or with transcription skills.

Writing intervention programs or support from special education or ESL colleagues can be helpful in some cases. In some classes, teachers can also use digital technologies such as speech-to-text software to support students who would benefit from additional assistance in communicating verbal ideas into print.

Writing development, however, includes more than effectively employing mechanics in one's writing. Composing skills must also be addressed and supported. This includes learning how to communicate the "what" of writing, as well as the "how" and "why." For adolescents, in particular, writing development should involve learning to select what words to choose or include, how to provide accurate and clear detail, and how to express thoughts in clear, creative, concise ways. Related to these skills, learners must understand the writing process and how to plan and/or brainstorm what to write as well as how to revise what one writes in terms of structure, organization, and content.

Writing development also includes understanding different genres (e.g., poetry, short stories, scripts, nutrition guides, theorems, equations, athletic contest rules) and the ways the elements of audience, purpose, and context influence a text's content, form, and style/mechanics (National Council of Teachers of English, 2018). Teachers can share their own approaches to writing by modeling a writing process while simultaneously explaining what they do when they research, plan, organize, edit, and revise their writing.

DEVELOPING AND SUPPORTING ADOLESCENTS' READING AND WRITING PROFICIENCY

It is important to know how humans' brains work and how humans learn to read and write because there are specific, discrete skills and knowledge that learners learn, remember, and apply. When learners have these skills, they can use them to decode (i.e., read) and encode (i.e., write). Becoming familiar with aspects of literacy skill development gives teachers a framework for understanding and identifying what adolescents might need regarding instructional reading and writing support and resources. Other considerations also come into play when employing a "yes, and" approach connected to adolescent reading and writing instruction and development. One is motivation.

Motivation and Engagement

Research demonstrates a connection between reading motivation, engagement, and achievement (Taboada et al., 2009). More than 20 years ago, Guthrie and Wigfield (2000) defined reading motivation as the "goals, values and beliefs concerning the topics, processes, and outcomes of reading" (p. 405). Motivation is complex and multifaceted. Extrinsic factors impact a student's motivation, such as social recognition, competition, and grades. Additionally, multiple intrinsic factors contribute to motivation, including feelings of competence, curiosity, degree of involvement in the reading and writing process, compliance, a willingness to read because reading is viewed as satisfying or rewarding, relatedness, and autonomy (Troyer, 2017). Adolescents can be motivated by the value they see in a text or a task (present or future), their self-perceptions of themselves as readers, and their perceived success in past reading experiences.

Thinking about reading and writing instruction as skill development thus also needs to include attention to motivation, particularly when working with adolescent learners. For adolescents, literacy instruction can't focus solely on skill development. Rather, skill development should occur within a larger framework that recognizes students' goals, values, interests, and beliefs as they relate to reading and writing. On a practical level, across and within conversations about decoding, schema, comprehension strategies, and vocabulary, it's important to pay attention to what is and isn't contributing to students' motivation to read and write. For example, supporting adolescent students' decoding or vocabulary skills also involves knowing and drawing on ideas and topics of interest that motivate them and empower them to draw on their background knowledge and expertise. A lack of cultural relevance in the texts they read and write, particularly for males and students of color, may inhibit students' ability to relate to the content, which may prompt them to disengage from assignments (Kirkland, 2011). Adolescents are more motivated to read and write when they see clear connections and value, as well as when they are interested in and can choose texts and/or tasks. Students must build their confidence to meet new literacy challenges. The more confident adolescents are as learners, the more likely they are to be engaged in their learning (Lent, 2009).

"Struggling" Readers and Writers

Although the terms "struggling reader" and "struggling writer" are used to refer to adolescents who aren't yet reading at grade level or who need additional support, we choose to use the phrase "not yet proficient," which implies expected growth and development. The reality is that many learners, at any age, "struggle" with particular aspects of reading and writing. And they do so for many reasons.

We worked recently with a beginning history teacher, who shared a story about a new 8th-grade student they worked with who appeared to be disengaged from a research-based assignment. The initial assumption was that the student simply didn't want to and/or didn't see value in doing the work. However, when the teacher engaged with the student one on one and asked questions, the student's responses made it clear that the real issue was that the student could not yet read and thus could not understand the assignment, let alone complete it independently.

In conversing with the student, the teacher also learned that the student had worked hard at a previous school to remain unnoticed in a classroom, not because they didn't want to learn but because they knew they didn't yet have enough skills and understanding to read and comprehend texts independently and were embarrassed about it. This student also felt uncomfortable asking for help because they knew teachers expected proficiency. The teacher shared with us that they were completely taken aback when they realized what this student needed and frustrated on the student's behalf that someone hadn't noticed and addressed this earlier. The teacher also explained that they had no idea how to help this student because they assumed that by the time students were in middle school they knew how to read and write.

Adolescents' literacy needs are varied and complex. Some adolescent learners are not yet proficient in decoding. This may be because of a reading disability or, for our English learners, because the language is new. Other adolescents are not yet proficient in reading particular texts because they lack the background knowledge to comprehend the information in that text. For others, it's the encounter with new vocabulary words they don't yet know or understand. They may lack strategies to draw on to make sense of or try to understand new words and concepts. Still other adolescents aren't sure how to navigate and make meaning of various discipline-specific texts, such as complicated musical scores, tables and charts, and highly technical explanations. Other adolescents know how to read but choose not to because of previous experiences with reading that haven't been meaningful or perhaps contributed to feelings of anxiety, shame, and failure.

As adolescents develop new literacy skills, productive struggle should be expected, welcomed, and supported. Adolescents need to think (and sometimes rethink) about what they're learning, and they need opportunities to practice and receive feedback. This feedback from teachers should include what to do when an adolescent doesn't yet understand and is not yet proficient when it comes to reading and writing. Learning to read and write takes time, and the process isn't always linear.

"YES, AND" APPROACH TO ADOLESCENTS' READING AND WRITING SKILLS

We know that the how and why of reading and writing instruction, including adolescent literacy instruction, is complicated and varied. As noted throughout this chapter, there have been and continue to be many discussions and debates about what "works" when it comes to reading and writing instruction. Literacy is associated with both general and specific skills, and literacy development is ongoing. Moreover, literacy instruction is the responsibility of all teachers.

In our work with beginning teachers, we recommend Dweck's (2008) work on growth mindset, which is the belief that a learner's abilities are developed through consistent dedication and hard work, including a commitment to try, fail, and try again. Adolescents' brains and talents are a starting point, and their capacity is developed when they and others believe they can succeed and when they have the resources they need to do so. A "yes, and" approach allows us to teach and support adolescents in their reading and writing development with a growth mindset as well as the idea that skill development needs to occur alongside fostering students' motivation, engagement, and background knowledge. When we understand students' reading and writing needs within and across subject areas, we can foster a love of learning, resilience, and feelings of confidence, relevancy, and importance. Doing so increases our capacity to teach and our students' capacity for learning and success.

MOVING FORWARD

Secondary teachers require a basic understanding of reading and writing to effectively support adolescents' learning and literacy development. When considering the necessary skills adolescents need to be proficient readers and writers, it can be easy to conclude that skill development is finite. Generally, it is assumed that if students achieve certain skills by a certain age or grade level, they will be proficient.

Literacy skills, however, are contextual. Depending on the context, different skills are needed for different purposes. It's thus important to remember that adolescents' literacy development is ongoing. While an adolescent might have an established base of phonics skills and vocabulary knowledge, they will continually encounter new words, texts, modes, and genres. In addition, their motivation and beliefs directly impact their engagement in their literacy development. Adolescents' reading and writing development depends on acquiring necessary skills, as well as extrinsic and intrinsic factors that contribute to their motivation to read and write. In the next chapter, we'll explore how knowing students and what matters to their identities in and out of school can support their literacy development.

Questions to Consider

- *Connected to stages of reading and writing, how might you support adolescents' literacy development in your subject area?*
- *How might you assess and identify students' literacy needs? What resources can you use to meet these needs?*
- *What role does motivation play in your students' interest in the texts and tasks within your subject area? How might you increase students' motivation and engagement with these texts and tasks?*

CHAPTER 3

Adolescents' Literacy Contexts and Practices

KEY TERMS

Academic literacy: the language and language structures used in school lessons, texts, assignments, and tests (also known as *academic language* or *academic English*)

Context: the situation in which something exists, happens, and/or gets applied. Connected to adolescent literacy development, this refers to the places, situations, and groups and identities within which humans acquire and use knowledge for specific purposes

People learn and use knowledge in many different contexts. In this chapter we explore an important factor that impacts and informs adolescents' literacy development—namely, the contexts in which adolescents' literacy skills and practices are developed and applied, which includes in- and out-of-school settings. We focus on two "yes, and" approaches to commonly held beliefs about literacy: that literacy development is ongoing, and that literacy is school-, home-, and community-based.

Though fundamental decoding and encoding skills can be applied to and in various contexts, not all contexts are the same. When, where, and how these skills are applied is impacted by where we are, why we are there, and who we are with. This means that school isn't the only place where learners develop and use literacy skills. In fact, humans approach a multitude of literacy skills, including reading and writing, differently depending on where they live, work, worship, and play (Christenbury et al., 2009; Gee, 2015a, 2015b; Hull & Shultz, 2002). Just as secondary teachers must understand what happens developmentally in learners' brains and bodies as they develop literacy skills, they also must recognize that learning and literacy development occurs within multiple contexts that inform how, when, and to what degree particular skills are developed, prioritized, and used.

CONTEXT

Context refers to the situation in which something exists, happens, and/or gets applied. Humans aren't born knowing how to bowl, garden, weave, sing, skateboard, surf, paint, or compose. Before we can participate in these activities, we must first learn the essential skills. At the same time, what and how we learn is informed by the contexts in which we reside. Sometimes we belong to communities because they are associated with our families' beliefs, values, and practices. Where we live also influences what we experience and are exposed to. If we don't live near an ocean or another large body of water with active waves, we are less likely to take up water sports and may have no experience with watercraft. Similarly, living in proximity to mountains presents opportunities to learn about and become skilled at skiing, hiking, and climbing. We are all born into and interact in particular contexts, with different social and cultural practices involving language, interactions around print texts, speaking, and listening.

For example, in the United States, migrant families and students' contexts differ from learners who are born into and grow up in the same community. Students growing up in rural, urban, and suburban areas have and operate in separate contexts, as well as those who travel regularly and those who may not have the resources to move beyond their home communities. Contexts differ because there exists a diversity of cultures, races, ethnicities, beliefs, languages, practices, and values. Within these contexts are also variations in geography, economy, and environment.

LITERACY IN CONTEXT

The idea of context as it relates to literacy development and learning more broadly is rooted in various scholars' work. Foregrounding the contexts in which literacy development occurs draws on theories from disciplines such as anthropology, psychology, and sociology (Hruby, 2001). Collectively known as sociocultural theories, a term that results from combining "social" and "cultural," this body of theories represents a variety of perspectives and emphases but overall asserts that reading and writing are elements of larger practices that are socially patterned and that these literacy practices are shaped by historical status and power relationships (Barton et al., 2000; Gee, 2015b; Street, 2001). This approach to literacy development focuses on human interactions in and around texts that happen within different contexts that include our lived experiences, social and cultural identities, and the knowledge and expertise within our communities. In addition to approaching literacy as a set of skills that an individual has or does not have, teachers must also understand that adolescents' literacy development is informed and influenced by what an individual does with others in and across multiple contexts (Moje & Lewis, 2007). So, although similarities exist in the cognitive processes that occur as learners develop literacy skills, such as reading and writing, this skill development and acquisition occurs in and across multiple contexts, in and out of academic settings.

Because context impacts literacy development, the ways we find and use recipes, how and where we shop, and what we do for entertainment reveal information about how we have learned to use literacy skills, including reading and writing for particular purposes. Conversations with adolescents reveal the various contexts in which they live, work, play, and learn. Adolescents come to school with multiple and meaningful interests, skills, experiences, and expertise they are excited about and committed to. Within their families, they might participate in different religious contexts where they read, hear, and respond to sacred texts, such as the Quran or the Bible. They might also use language differently with their families than in school contexts. They might interact on social media platforms with their friends, speaking and writing in different ways than in their conversations with adults or in their places of employment.

Russian philosopher Lev Vygotsky (1978) studied how children learned new skills, noting that "children's learning begins long before they attend school . . . Any learning a child encounters in school always has a previous history" (p. 84). As a way to explain how learners learn, Vygotsky created the idea of a "zone of proximal development," a concept rooted in the social nature of learning, including the need for learners to have access to "more experienced others" (i.e., those with more experience, understanding, knowledge, and skills). In school settings, teachers are considered "more experienced others" because they have more experience and knowledge than their students, specifically related to the academic knowledge and skills students are expected to learn.

Vygotsky's (1978) zone of proximal development suggests that differences exist between what a learner can do without help and what they can achieve with guidance and encouragement from a more experienced other. In addition to a learner being ready and able to learn, "human learning presupposes a specific social nature and a process by which children grow into the intellectual life of those around them" (p. 88). In other words, learning—including humans' literacy development and acquisition—is socially constructed and centered in learners' particular contexts while also aided by more experienced others in those contexts, which include nonacademic as well as academic-oriented situations.

> **LITERACY IN CONTEXT: SKATEBOARDING EXAMPLE**
>
> Let's consider a literacy practice outside of school context—skateboarding. Just because someone identifies as a skateboarder, it doesn't mean they are proficient or have mastered particular tricks or moves. Like the skills needed to develop as proficient readers and writers, skateboarders must also learn basic skills to operate a skateboard. They will likely use different strategies and resources as they develop proficiency. Like reading and writing, skateboarding is a learned set of skills acquired and applied over time, with much practice and with the guidance of other more experienced skateboarders. In addition, although specific skills and knowledge are associated with skateboarding, a person learns how to skateboard within a specific context, with different tools and resources, and usually in a community that includes others interested in skateboarding.

Learning to use and acquire knowledge within a particular context occurs informally by watching and doing rather than being formally taught or taught in isolation. Over the years, we've employed the concept of an apprenticeship when explaining how and why learning, including literacy development, is not only skill based but also rooted in social interaction. By definition, an apprenticeship is a period of time in which someone learns a skill or trade from an expert. Using the idea of an apprenticeship (Vygotsky, 1978), the literacy skills and practices humans learn within particular contexts outside academic settings are learned through watching, learning, applying, and doing. When we consider apprenticeship models in trade jobs such as carpentry and electrical work, it refers to how novices work alongside experts and learn from them while doing the work. In the same way, many of us have learned literacy skills, values, attitudes, and beliefs within particular contexts from more experienced others within those contexts.

When exploring when, where, and how humans learn and become literate, some scholars use terms such as "communities of practice" (Lave & Wenger, 1991), "networks" (Moje, 2008), "out-of-school literacies" (Hull & Schultz, 2002), and "funds of knowledge" (González et al., 2005). Additionally, connected to literacy development, earlier scholars have used terms such as "literacy practices" (Street, 1995) and "literacy events" (Heath, 1983) when examining literacy skill development and acquisition within a particular group, location, and/or culture. These can be useful terms for exploring aspects of literacy development, and we share this research with beginning teachers to provide a broad overview of how and why context matters and why teachers must understand the impact of contexts on adolescents' literacy development.

Literacy as Discourse

Within multiple contexts, there are different ways of acting, interacting, valuing, feeling, dressing, thinking, behaving, believing, and so on. In the field of literacy research, this has been described as "discourses" (Gee, 2015a, 2015b), a concept that refers to all the ways of being within particular social and cultural groups. The concept of discourses showcases how humans learn the values and practices of various contexts in which they live, which becomes part of how they act, see, and think (Lewis et al., 2007). Context, then, is part of who we are and how we identify ourselves.

For example, the discourse we use in a job interview will likely differ from the one we use at a bar on Saturday night, which likely differs from the one used in church on Sunday morning. Even in school, students' conversations in the cafeteria with their peers differ from those conversations they likely engage in with their teacher during their 3rd-hour AP geology course or on the wrestling mat after school.

With respect to reading, a Christian fundamentalist, for example, will read the Torah (the first five books of the Bible: Genesis, Exodus, Leviticus, Numbers, Deuteronomy) in very different ways and for different purposes than would a practicing Orthodox Jew. Although these two people read the same text and use the same cognitive processes to do so, including decoding and comprehending, because of the difference in their contexts, they will likely read and understand the text in different ways. In fact, they will likely interact with and generate different meanings from the text, which may lead to individual applications.

Discourses vary in writing, as well. For example, adolescents are not likely to text their friends and grandparents using the same words, emojis, and slang. How and what they post to social media sites, including the rhetorical choices they make, differs from a historical analysis they may write or a lab report they produce. Context and audience matter, even when texting.

Literacy Contexts Are Not Neutral

The contexts in which we live, work, play, and learn highlight the ways literacy is not neutral. Some contexts and their related literacy skills have more power and privilege than others. School-based literacy skills acquired in academic settings, for example, are the currency of jobs, colleges, and universities (to name a few), although academic contexts represent but one of many contexts in which adolescents exist. Given the importance of the cognitive skills needed for literacy development, a recognition of the contexts in which these skills are developed acknowledges the cultural, social, historical, and economic practices valued within a given context (Baker-Bell, 2020; Gee, 2015b; Lankshear & Knobel, 2007).

In her examination of historical and current practices in schools and curricula within the United States, Muhammad (2020) explains how literacy practices are informed, influenced, and patterned by social institutions and power relationships. This means that, depending on the context, some literacies and literacy practices are more dominant, visible, and influential than others. More than 40 years ago, Heath (1983), a longtime researcher in the field, offered a powerful illustration of power and privilege related to literacy evidenced through bedtime stories. Reading and/or listening to bedtime stories is a literacy practice some children and families engage in, but not all. Heath found in her research that many White, middle-upper-class children routinely experience and participate in a bedtime story routine with parents or other family members. This routine included reading books aloud regularly as part of a child's bedtime routine. In other families, however, this was not typical practice.

This example matters because many teachers, administrators, politicians, and policymakers prioritize certain literacy practices routines, such as the bedtime story. While we don't expect adolescents to have books read to them by caregivers in the evenings before they go to bed, teachers may assume and expect that adolescents come to their subject matter classes having had certain home-based literacy experiences, including visiting libraries, engaging in read-alouds, traveling, and having sustained, purposeful conversations with peers and adults in which they communicate ideas, feelings, emotions, events and stories.

Literacy has always been connected with issues of power because the literacies we experience and express are informed, influenced, and patterned by social institutions and power relationships (Lewis et al., 2007). Those who have historically held social and political power in a society determine which types of literacies are considered valid and worth teaching and measuring (Emdin, 2016; Muhammad, 2020). Moreover, who has access to what resources and what is valued continues to be evident in education and economic policy decisions (Baker-Bell, 2020; Paris & Alim, 2017).

Paris (2012) explains how dominant literacy, language, and cultural practices in the United States, historically and still today, disproportionately advantage and disadvantage different groups of learners. Paris's work notes that the historical challenges different groups in the United States have faced when those with power and privilege devalue certain groups' contexts, including experiences and expertise practiced and gained in non-White, middle-class settings and contexts. This includes the expectations for academic language and the types of texts students have had access to. When privileging particular practices and skills defined and used by dominant mainstream groups, institutions and governments can end up devaluing or ignoring students' contexts (Baker-Bell, 2020; Kendi, 2019; Millar & Warrican, 2015).

Additionally, access to academic literacy support and education can be a form of power in and of itself. Individuals or groups who have access to high-performing schools and reside in affluent, resourced communities are better equipped to navigate complex social, economic, and political systems. This frequently translates to having additional access and opportunity, including access to higher-paying jobs, resources, and opportunities. On the other hand, individuals or groups who possess fewer resources and reside in underfunded and/or underresourced communities face barriers to achieving power and influence, as they may struggle to navigate complex systems and may have limited venues in which to share their ideas, positions, and beliefs.

Those in power determine which literacies and associated practices are more or less valuable. These determinations also inform what is included or excluded from schools, academic curricula, and mainstream societal norms (Emdin, 2016; Kay, 2018). A recent example can be seen in the College Board's new advanced placement curriculum for African American studies, which underwent multiple changes after politicians voiced concern and exerted influence to change the originally approved curriculum (Hartocollis & Fawcett, 2023). In its final published form, the course curriculum lacks what many consider important aspects of the African American experience, presenting a narrowed understanding of the rich and complex history of Africans who came to the United States against their will (Hartocollis & Fawcett, 2023). Limiting students' access to ideas and subject matter also impacts, and in some cases limits, their literacy development.

Academic Literacy and Academic Settings

When context is centered on academic settings, there's an assumption that literacy is neutral. This idea is supported by a perspective that says literacy is a set of finite skills, readily and equally available to all students, in all contexts. In the United States, this is based on the idea that all learners have access to and participate in some sort of K–12 educational experience and that these experiences are all relatively the same and provide the same opportunities and access for learners. However, this idea unravels when we consider the following questions:

- Who gets to decide which literacy skills are "right"?
- Who determines which literacy skills get taught, measured, and assessed in schools?

- What texts and whose perspectives do students have access to as they develop their literacy skills?

Academic literacy is most closely aligned with current dominant mainstream sociocultural group contexts, namely, middle- and upper-middle-class White people (Baker-Bell, 2020; Emdin, 2016; Kay, 2018). The literacy skills in these contexts are thus often viewed as "correct" or "best" (Muhammad, 2020). Literacy skills in other contexts aren't viewed as such and thus do not carry the same power or privilege. For example, consider the negative stereotypes of people who do not speak standard or academic English. Although Appalachian English, Southern American English, and Black English are rule-governed systems with complex grammatical features, many people assume that speakers of these dialects are uneducated. While we know this to be categorically false, the assumption persists in some places even today. It thus becomes imperative that teachers know how to support adolescents' literacy development, in the fullest sense, including fostering their understanding of the power and privilege afforded by various contexts.

Another consequence of privileging academic literacy and the literacy skills defined and practiced by dominant mainstream sociocultural groups in particular academic contexts is that institutions and governments that give power to and fund schools overtly or subversively devalue or ignore students' other literacies, which are not recognized or valued in academic settings (Kendi, 2019; Millar & Warrican, 2015; Price-Dennis & Muhammad, 2021). As Muhammad (2020) explains in her exploration of Black literary societies and the implications these societies have on teaching and learning today, there is power associated with being literate because it provides access to information, which expands opportunities and understanding. As teachers committed to supporting adolescents' literacy development, we must also ensure students' access to a wide variety of texts and information.

Additionally, when we seek to measure adolescents' literacy within academic contexts, especially with standardized assessments, we need to recognize how these tests support and promote specific definitions and understandings of literacy and language practices. Research has demonstrated that standardized tests do not consider many Black, Indigenous, and People of Color students' linguistic and cultural backgrounds and expertise (Baker-Bell, 2020). English learners, for example, may possess a deep understanding of ideas and subject matter but may not yet be proficient in the language of instruction. Their knowledge and understanding cannot be measured on tests written in a language in which they are not proficient. Moreover, it is unfair to expect English Learners to learn subject matter at the same rate as native speakers because

English Learners are simultaneously learning a new language (Nora & Echevarria, 2016).

> **BLACK ENGLISH BIAS**
>
> Clearly, literacy affords power and privilege. In fact, in a recent study, Robinson and Norton (2019) found that Black children in 14 states were over-represented in speech and language impairment categories because the language tests used were biased against Black English. These tests included incorrect answers that used grammatical features found within Black English that in this context would be correct. This raises many questions, including what are these tests truly measuring, and how are such limited data used to perpetuate false narratives about certain groups of adolescents and their literacy skills? In this situation, Black children who speak Black English are over-diagnosed with speech impairments. In contrast, Black children may also be underdiagnosed for speech impairments when test givers do not have a proper understanding of how the children test, talk, and communicate with others.

ADOLESCENTS' LITERACY PRACTICES IN CONTEXT

What some adolescents do in contexts other than school can feel and look so different from school-based literacy tasks and skills that these students don't necessarily realize all the knowledge and skills they bring with them to their secondary classrooms (Muhammad, 2020, 2023). Many adolescents' home and community literacy experiences are not included in the school curriculum or recognized as valued literacy skills within academic settings. This is lamentable. Acknowledging, naming, and recognizing these contexts can draw attention to what motivates and gives adolescents purpose and meaning when it comes to learning and communicating. Taking an asset-based approach (Dweck, 2008) accounts for the importance of context as it relates to adolescent literacy development, positively impacting how teachers and their students view what adolescents know, do, and can do. Acknowledging and affirming the importance of context also encourages teachers to further support students' learning in school, particularly when teachers purposefully and regularly draw on these contexts, including the experiences and expertise students have, as they support adolescents' literacy development (Christenbury et al., 2009; González et al., 2005).

> **TEACHERS' CONTEXTS, EXPERIENCES, AND EXPERTISE**
>
> To support adolescents' literacy development in academic settings, teachers must recognize that adolescents, like all humans, navigate and experience different contexts, and these contexts matter a great deal. When we ask beginning teachers to reflect on the various contexts they have been and/or are a part of, they share their passions, experiences, interests, and abilities—many of which have little to do with their teaching career. The number of beginning teachers who are sports and outdoor enthusiasts, bakers, chefs, martial artists, and gamers, as well as musicians and theater buffs, never ceases to amaze us.
>
> It's especially fun when someone shares information about a context or experience that is new to the rest of the group. For example, one of us worked with a new teacher who was a rock climber. This individual's expertise enabled the entire class to learn more about bouldering, lead climbing, and top roping. Moreover, as we noted in the previous chapter, not only did this educator need to learn and apply the skills associated with rock climbing, they were also motivated and interested to learn. Additionally, the contexts in which they found themselves, including belonging to a rock-climbing club, having economic resources to support this interest, and having ready access to indoor climbing walls and outdoor terrain, supported their ability to learn and become a skilled rock climber.

In addition to supporting adolescents' literacy skill development through an asset-based approach, having adolescents share their interests affirms the various contexts in which they learn and invites them to share their participation in popular culture phenomena. These can help secondary students make connections between multiple contexts and what they are learning, reading, and writing in academic settings. Doing so fosters and acknowledges the multiple ways students are literate and become literate—in and out of school. This can be hard, though, particularly as many contexts and their associated practices and norms may not be familiar to teachers. That said, valuing adolescents' contexts matters, which means teachers need to remain actively curious about their students' contexts, experiences, and expertise (Muhammad, 2023). We must assume students come to each subject area and every class with expertise and valuable experiences, and it's our job to identify what these are and empower adolescents to see themselves as learners and as possessing expertise upon which they can build and extend. To do so, explicit connections between students' academic and non-academic contexts must be made. Specifically, teachers must partner with their students to recognize, understand, and integrate the contexts in which these students live, play, work, and learn.

ACKNOWLEDGING AND VALUING ADOLESCENTS' LITERACY CONTEXTS AND PRACTICES

Acknowledging and valuing students' varied literacy contexts and practices can happen in many ways. Sometimes teachers learn by asking students questions, other times by listening to conversations and making observations. For various reasons, including what we know about adolescent development, adolescents will differ in how much information they share with others, including teachers. We don't need to know everything about every student, but it's important to remain curious and actively elicit information when and where possible. There are many resources available when it comes to questions to ask adolescents. These can be used as ice-breakers at the beginning of a school year or semester, as well as an ongoing practice to actively build communities of learners within a given classroom. Additionally, it's important to allow space for students to choose what and how much they want to share, and not every question will resonate with students. That's okay, too. The goal of asking questions is to begin recognizing and understanding students' contexts, including their experiences and expertise. There are no magical, one-size-fits-all questions. But, asking questions can be a good start to recognizing and understanding adolescents' contexts.

> **QUESTIONS TO ASK STUDENTS TO LEARN ABOUT THEIR VARIOUS CONTEXTS**
>
> Although teachers can use an existing literacy-based attitude/interests assessment (there are a number of them), some questions beginning teachers we've worked with have used with their students include the following:
> - What's the app or website you use most and why?
> - What's something you'd like to learn how to do?
> - What's something you're good at? How did you learn this?
> - What's something you can teach someone else to do?
> - What and who is on your playlist and/or watchlist right now?
> - What's something adults don't understand about tweens/teens?
> - What is one of the hardest things you've ever done (or learned) and why?
> - What are the qualities of a good friend?
> - What would make you jump out of bed at 6 A.M. on a Saturday?
> - If you could drop or change one thing in your life without consequence, what would it be and why?
> - If money were not a factor, what would you do after graduation? Why?
> - Who has a cool or interesting job? Why do you think so?

Of course, not all questions make sense in all subject areas. Knowing the socially based nature of adolescents' literacy skill development and how humans engage in literacy practices in various contexts can be helpful because it allows teachers to incorporate these experiences and expertise into their classrooms and curricula.

Jerasa and Boffone (2021) offer suggestions for teachers who are interested in integrating the social media site TikTok into their classrooms. For English Language Arts teachers, these researchers suggest utilizing #Booktok (via TikTok) to capitalize on adolescents' expertise with TikTok. Students can draw on their understanding of the social media site's cultural norms and ways users share ideas, communicate with others, and respond to others' TikTok posts. Integrating this site into the classroom and ELA curriculum invites students' social media practices, at least those associated with this site, into their experiences with reading and responding to literature.

An experienced high school history teacher we know purposefully spends time getting to know her students' music interests and asks them to tell her about the artists and songs they listen to. Using this information, this teacher then makes explicit connections to these artists and genres when talking about the importance of knowing the historical context of texts, particularly a historian's responsibility to understand larger cultural influences on events and to situate people and movements within specific periods. Similarly, a physics teacher could use a student's interest and/or expertise in rock climbing to share information about Newton's third law (i.e., if object 1 applies force to object 2, object 2 applies an equal and opposite force to object 1). And a physical education teacher might draw on the same student's interest in rock climbing to further students' understanding of aerobic and anaerobic activity (rock climbing involves both).

In our work with beginning teachers around recognizing and understanding adolescents' literacy contexts and practices, we regularly reference Muhammad's (2020) framework for approaching literacy instruction. Rooted in the historical and cultural realities of Black students, Muhammad identifies four pursuits on which to build and design curriculum across subject areas that include students' identities, skills, intellect, and criticality. In Muhammad's (2023) more recent exploration of how students' contexts can be used to inform and support students' learning and literacy development, she includes the necessity of a fifth pursuit: joy. She notes that we must embed joy as part of teaching and learning. Joy is centered on aspects of wellness, healing, beauty, justice, and healing for ourselves, our communities, and our world. Connecting joy to students' learning supports and grows their interest and motivation and enables them to see how the contexts in which they live, work, play, and learn are connected. Students begin to see themselves, including their experiences and expertise, as having value in the academic settings they inhabit.

Different contexts have had more or less power and privilege over time in the United States (and in most other places in the world). Muhammad thus challenges teachers to name and acknowledge students' cultural and historical realities and contexts as a way of claiming and affirming the value of their communities and contexts. Doing so enhances teachers' ability to recognize, understand, and integrate students' lived experiences and expertise, giving them a powerful purpose to learn and contribute to the world.

INTEGRATING ADOLESCENTS' LITERACY CONTEXTS AND PRACTICES

Integration of students' contexts also means teachers can draw on their students' existing skills and build on them as they support their students in meeting course objectives and outcomes. The more teachers choose to recognize, understand, and integrate adolescents' contexts, the more they will learn about their students' expertise, interests, and experiences. Doing so means that teachers and their students will be more likely to make connections between the skills they develop in and across contexts and the content and skills they learn in academic settings.

As noted previously, integrating adolescents' varied contexts will likely differ across subject areas. Using a "yes, and" approach when it comes to understanding and integrating students' context, adolescents have opportunities to integrate their social and academic worlds (Christenbury et al., 2009). Sociocultural theorists encourage teachers to purposefully draw on what they know about their students' various contexts when reviewing and/or introducing new concepts and texts. They also remind us to remember that it's important to understand how adolescents' contexts can and should be integrated to support their literacy development and academic success. Further, as noted in Chapter 2, it's essential to teach specific skills and strategies when fostering and supporting learners' literacy development. Teachers must acknowledge the value of skills and contexts and actively seek to embed academic skills and knowledge within students' contexts.

For a study focused on adolescent males' various contexts outside academic settings, Deb interviewed a teenager who hated his English Language Arts class. It was clear through this interview that he did not identify as a writer or reader and was not engaged in or motivated by class assignments. He was, however, highly motivated by participating in his church and spent 4 nights a week doing church-related activities. One of these activities involved writing weekly song lyrics for his youth group, which he and a group of musicians performed during the Sunday church service. We wonder what might have changed if his teacher had known of his interest in songwriting. Perhaps he would have been further supported in making these connections and would have understood the overlap of literacy skills and content connections in both contexts. Perhaps his songs could have been shared, perhaps even further developed, as part of the creative writing process.

Avoiding Appropriation

As we've already stated, secondary teachers should bridge what adolescents know and do outside of academic settings with the skills and knowledge they need and learn in school. However, we also realize this can be complicated and could, unintentionally, lead to issues of appropriating particular adolescents' cultures, identities, and practices, particularly when different contexts afford adolescents different levels of power and privilege (Baker-Bell, 2020; Kendi, 2019; Muhammad, 2020). The appropriation of particular adolescents' cultures, identities, and practices is complex and can have negative effects on individuals and the broader cultural groups they identify with and/or represent. Appropriation occurs when people from dominant cultural groups, for the purpose of personal gain or to appear fashionable, adopt aspects of another culture without understanding or respecting their cultural significance. For adolescents, this type of appropriation can be particularly harmful, as well as hurtful, as it may impact their developing sense of identity and self. Additionally, adolescents may feel pressure to conform to a dominant culture to fit in, which may lead to a loss of cultural identity and a disconnection from their heritage. Cultural appropriation also contributes to the erasure and distortion of marginalized cultures and people and serves to perpetuate harmful and hurtful stereotypes.

For example, a teacher in a predominantly White school is teaching a unit on Native American culture. The teacher decides to ask students to wear and/or dress up in traditional Native American clothing for the day. The teacher does not consult with Native American students or community members before making this decision. As a result, the students who are not Native American dress in a way they are told is intended to be fun and festive and focused on learning. However, the instructor has taken something sacred to Native American culture—in this instance, clothing and dress—and used it for their own purposes. In doing so, although the instructor's intention may have been good, they show no respect for the history and traditions of Native American culture. Other examples of appropriation include using a student's cultural or racial background as a punchline in a joke, or making assumptions about a student's abilities based on their culture, gender, or race.

To address this issue, particularly as we think about the various contexts in which adolescents live and learn, it is important for teachers to promote cultural understanding and respect, particularly among adolescents still developing their sense of self and identity. Teachers must get to know their students, including the knowledge, skills, and identities they bring to the classroom. Moreover, teachers must be educated and teach their students about cultural appropriation and its impacts, as well as support and engage in efforts to name and amplify marginalized cultural voices and practices. Ultimately, fostering a culture of respect and inclusivity in the classroom is one step toward mitigating the harm and hurt caused by cultural appropriation, while also promoting adolescents' awareness, understanding, and appreciation of diverse cultures, including those they themselves represent as well as their peers' cultures and contexts.

"YES, AND" APPROACH TO ADOLESCENTS' LITERACY CONTEXTS AND PRACTICES

When we think about adolescents' multiple contexts, as well as the ways in which their out-of-school literacy experiences and the skills, practices, and expertise are developed in beyond-school contexts, beginning teachers ask us how to account for this knowledge and these skills. Many times, these are not the practices assessed in school, and sometimes these practices, skills, and expertise don't easily translate to academic literacy practices. Acknowledging and inviting students' out-of-school literacy practices into secondary classrooms and subject areas, though, can provide valuable insights into adolescents' reading and writing skills, interests, and practices.

Here are some steps suggestions for how to assess students' out-of-school literacy contexts and practices:

- Conduct surveys or interviews (e.g., what they like to read, how often they read, what types of writing they do, how they access and consume information, and where and how they get reading materials).
- Ask for samples of their writing (e.g., patrons' orders from a restaurant, texts between friends, social media posts, notes they write, journal entries, and work orders). Of course, it's important for students to be able to discern what is considered appropriate texts for this task, which offers opportunities to talk with students about what writing is and what constitutes a piece of writing.
- Encourage students to document and share their literacy habits (e.g., ask students to generate lists of the texts they read, write, listen to, and view throughout a given day).
- Invite students to analyze their or others' social media profiles (e.g., ask students to review age-appropriate social profiles, posts, and forums and consider the ideas shared, positionality of

influencers, and the words and images used and why). Note that not all students will have access to or interest in social media, so other genres such as digital, print, and video advertisements may also be useful.

Overall, when seeking to learn more about adolescents' literacy contexts and practices, the goal is to gather as much information as possible about students to better understand their needs, abilities, interests, and expertise as thinkers, readers, and writers. This information can then be used to develop effective literacy instruction and support in and across subject areas.

MOVING FORWARD

As teachers, we must commit to actively learning about the different contexts in which adolescents live, work, play, and learn. When we do this, we utilize a "yes, and" approach to commonly held beliefs about literacy, namely, that literacy development is ongoing and literacy is school-, home-, and community-based. Approaching literacy as a social practice gives us language to recognize, value, integrate, and help bridge adolescents' interests, passions, and experiences to school contexts. Doing so helps us see our adolescent students holistically and be more aware of their diverse experiences and expertise in every classroom and school, which can help increase adolescents' confidence in what they can learn and accomplish across contexts. It also empowers teachers to frame and adapt subject matter to connect to the multiple and rich contexts in which students live and work.

Questions to Consider

- *What contexts do you identify with? What literacy practices are employed in these contexts?*
- *With which contexts do your students' identify? What practices are associated with these contexts?*
- *Given the subject area you teach, how might you recognize, understand, and integrate students' contexts and out-of-school literacy practices?*

CHAPTER 4

Identifying and Using Texts

KEY TERMS

Texts: print-based, aural, visual, spatial, gestural, or multimodal ways of using language, images, or symbols to communicate meaning to others

Text complexity: how easy or hard a text is for someone to read and understand as determined by qualitative and quantitative measures and reader and task factors

In this chapter, we explore the concept of "text" and how to support adolescent learners as they consume and create texts across subject areas. Texts, particularly at the secondary level, have varying degrees of complexity and pose numerous challenges. Thus, knowing what literacy skills a text requires of its adolescent reader, writer, listener, or viewer is important. Furthermore, there are many texts and ways to use texts with students to introduce, practice, and review subject area content. In highlighting this, we offer a "yes, and" approach to two commonly held literacy beliefs: that literacy is more than just reading, and that literacy development is ongoing. Texts can be more than just print based, and the literacy skills we need to understand these varied texts must be continually developed.

IDENTIFYING TEXTS

Historically, the word "text" has been used to describe print- and paper-based texts that use the written word to convey meaning, such as books and journals. When used in school contexts, "text" often refers to the subject area textbooks and books used with students. Since our definition of literacy involves more than just reading and writing, our definition of a text is broader. A text uses language, images, or symbols to communicate meaning. The particular mode or form of a text conveys meaning in particular ways (Kress, 2010). In other words, texts can be print based, aural, visual, spatial, gestural, or multimodal. If we can look at, watch, listen to, or create something that uses written words, images, layout, speech, sound, and movement, this is a text (The New London Group, 2000; Cope & Kalantzis, 2009). For example, a visual text will draw on visual elements such as line, color, spacing, texture, and placement to communicate meaning. Gestural texts rely on physical gestures, movements, and body language to convey meaning (Table 4.1).

To understand the meaning expressed in a text, we need to be familiar with what kind of text it is, along with its intended audience, medium, structures, features, and purpose. Returning to our conversation in Chapter 2 about literacy skills, we need skills specific to the kind of mode a text is. We must know how to decode words to make sense of a print-based text. To understand a visual text requires a general sense of how images convey meaning. When listening to an aural text that is spoken or sung, we need to understand types of sound and how sound or dynamics are used to convey meaning.

It's remarkable to consider the sheer variety of texts in our lives, and all that we already know about using these varied texts. Throughout our day, for example, we read, listen to, or watch many texts, and we also write, speak, and use images to create our own texts. We consume and create texts daily related to our interests, hobbies, or work experiences. Adolescents are no different. Consider a typical morning in the life of one

Table 4.1. Different Textual Modes and Examples

Mode	Definition	Examples
Print	Communicate meaning through the written word	Books, textbooks, newspaper and journal articles, poems, primary and secondary sources, story problems
Aural	Use audio or sound to communicate meaning	Podcasts, music recordings, audiobooks, radio broadcasts, voice messages, conversations
Visual	Communicate meaning through visual elements such as images and videos	Photographs, billboards, cartoons, fine art
Spatial	Use space and spatial relationships to communicate meaning	Maps, diagrams, blueprints, floor plans, sketches
Gestural	Convey meaning through physical gestures	Dance, sign language, miming, silent films
Multimodal	Use multiple modes to communicate meaning	Graphic novels, comics, posters, movies, interactive webpages, virtual reality

teenager. Ka'niya wakes up and checks her phone. She plays her favorite music albums on Spotify and sings along with the lyrics. As she gets dressed, she scrolls through her friends' SnapChat snaps and stories and responds to several of them before heading to the kitchen for breakfast. As she eats, Ka'niya texts her dad, who has already left for work, to see if he can pick her up after school. She then adds some food items to her family's grocery list before heading off to school. On her way out, she grabs the landscape crew job application she completed last night so she can turn it in after school.

Before she even enters a school building, Ka'niya interacts with many texts. She's learned to read, write, view, and understand these texts differently based on their mode, audience, and purpose. As discussed in the previous chapter, much of this out-of-school knowledge is overlooked or undervalued in school contexts. This is unfortunate because many of these texts involve skills and expertise that can be used as starting points for or bridges to school-based texts. In addition, many of these texts directly connect with adolescents' interests and experiences. Encountering texts is a central aspect of what happens in school, but it's important to remember that these school-based texts are only some of the many texts in adolescents' lives.

When we introduce the concept of text to beginning teachers, we highlight two main interactions with texts: consuming and creating. These terms differentiate between encountering a text created by someone else and creating a text ourselves.

Consuming and Creating Texts

We use the term "consuming" to refer to reading, listening to, or watching texts, and "creating" to refer to generating or curating words, images, sounds, or movements to convey meaning.

The ways we consume a text are influenced by a text's purpose, audience, and genre and our familiarity with it. For example, in the category of print-based texts, we read a tax form differently than we read a love letter, a smartphone text exchange with emojis, or a grocery list. We might skim a tax form to get a general idea of its layout and structure, read the instructions and definitions carefully to understand the terms used on the form, and review the information requested on the form to help us gather all the necessary documents and information. Accuracy and attention to detail guide our interactions with this text. On the other hand, we might read a love letter slowly, taking time to savor the words and expressions used. We might reflect on the feelings and intentions behind the words and analyze literary devices or techniques, such as metaphors, allusions, or repetition. Reading this kind of text is often an emotional, personal experience.

In the same way, we "read" visual texts like political cartoons differently than we read an advertisement or meme. A political cartoon typically uses satire or caricature to comment on political or social issues and relies on visual metaphors or symbolism to convey its meaning. We might need to read a political cartoon several times or look up information to understand the humor, images, and accompanying captions or dialogue. YouTube videos, on the other hand, rely on music, text, and effects to convey meaning. Because YouTube videos are typically created and viewed for entertainment, they can usually be understood quickly and easily.

We don't just consume texts but also create them. From sending text messages to writing song lyrics, filling out job applications, and posting social media images and content, we create or produce many texts daily. We've learned, in formal and informal ways, how to modify what we create based on the mode, structure, features, audience, and purpose. For example, we write emails differently than we write Instagram posts, poems, or text messages. In school contexts, we write a lab report differently than a history essay or a chart documenting our weekly exercise. The intended audience of a text also contributes to how we read or interact with it. Returning to our tax form example, we would need to read the form differently if it were intended to be read by tax professionals or by the general public. In the same way, a love letter would be written differently if it was for a specific person or a wider audience. Additionally, if we were the recipient of the love letter, we would read it differently than if it were written to someone else.

We share these examples to show how basic literacy skills, such as being able to decode words and make sense of sound dynamics or an image, can take us only so far in being able to interpret and make sense of a text. We also need to know how to interpret texts based on their specific purposes, audiences, and genres. While most adolescents have acquired the skills of decoding and encoding words, there is still much for them to learn about the texts they encounter in school and beyond, particularly because of how texts become increasingly complex in middle and high school. When we encounter a new kind of text or one more complex than what we are used to, we must develop skills so we can learn to make sense of it.

CONSIDERING THE COMPLEXITY OF TEXTS

It's important to consider not just the modes of texts that we use with students but also the difficulties present, or not, within these texts. Simply put, some texts are easier to understand than others. Difficult texts require more involvement from their intended audience. As we consider the skill development adolescents need to comprehend increasingly difficult texts, it's important for secondary teachers to recognize the factors that contribute to a text's complexity. When we can identify these factors, we can better support students in their understanding of texts.

The idea of text complexity isn't new; it has been used in the field of literacy for a long time. However, the publication of the Common Core State Standards in 2010 popularized the term with its emphasis on how students should be reading texts appropriately complex for their grade level. Since then, text complexity has become an important part of literacy instruction and assessment in the United States and beyond. In the following sections, we discuss aspects of text complexity as it relates to print-based and non-print-based texts.

PRINT-BASED TEXTS

Used to refer to print-based texts, the concept of text complexity is important for all secondary teachers to understand across grade levels and subject areas not only because of how subject area texts increase in their complexity in middle and high school but also because complex texts are everywhere. Helping adolescents become college and career ready means they need to be equipped to read the complex texts they will encounter in the workplace and/or in higher education. To achieve this, adolescents need access to and time spent learning how to understand complex texts.

In print-based texts, the vocabulary used, the structures of sentences, and the use of various text structures can present challenges to the reader. These features can make a text more difficult to synthesize, summarize, or comprehend. When readers encounter more complex texts, they must spend more time reading or thinking about these texts to comprehend their meaning. In other words, complex texts require a different kind of interaction than those print-based texts that are already familiar and/or are easier to understand.

Various subject area standards, such as the Common Core State Standards (CCSS), NextGen Science standards, American Council on the Teaching of Foreign Languages standards (ACTFL), and the National Core Arts Standards (NCAS), emphasize the importance of introducing adolescent learners to complex print-based texts and helping them develop the skills needed to comprehend and create these texts. For example, the NCAS standards relating to Arts as Communication support students' development in reading and writing complex texts (National Coalition for Core Arts Standards, 2014). The ACTFL standards outline five levels of proficiency, ranging from Novice to Distinguished, each of which is characterized by specific language abilities and skills (American Council on the Teaching of Foreign Languages, 2012). As learners progress through these levels, they can better comprehend and analyze more complex texts.

According to the CCSS (National Governors Association Center for Best Practices & Council of Chief State School Officers, 2010), college and career readiness requires students to be able to comprehend and analyze complex texts across a range of disciplines, including literature, science, history, and social studies. These texts contain challenging vocabulary, sophisticated sentence structures, and abstract concepts that require students to engage in higher-order thinking and draw on a wide range of background knowledge and reading strategies. The CCSS argue that reading complex texts helps students build language and literacy skills, and develop critical thinking and problem-solving abilities as well as a deeper appreciation for the complexities of language and culture. Exposure to complex texts and learning the skills involved in reading them helps students learn to analyze and evaluate arguments, synthesize information from multiple sources, and apply their understanding to real-world situations. The CCSS's three-part model for measuring text complexity highlights three factors to consider when thinking about text complexity: quantitative measures, qualitative measures, and reader and task factors. In our work with beginning teachers around texts, we find it helpful to refer to this three-part model.

Quantitative Measures of Print-Based Texts

Quantitative features of a text are the features that can be counted. This includes the length of words used, the number of syllables in the words used, word frequency, and sentence length and structure. Better measured by algorithms than by human readers, several factors help determine the quantitative features of texts (Table 4.2).

Readability formulas such as Accelerated Reader, ATOS levels, Lexile Analyzer, and the Fry Readability Formula, as well as features in Word and Google documents, can quantitatively measure text complexity. To

Table 4.2. Selected Quantitative Measures of Print-Based Texts

Quantitative Text Measures	Considerations
Word Length and Number of Syllables	Short versus long words (e.g., "mess" versus "catastrophe")
Number of Syllables in Words	Words with few syllables versus multisyllabic words (e.g., "big" versus "enormous")
Sentence Structure and Length	Straightforward and short versus long and complex (e.g., "Adolescents who read more have better literacy skills" versus "Research has shown that adolescents who engage in frequent and varied reading practices, whether it be for leisure or academic purposes, tend to develop stronger literacy skills over time, which positively impacts their academic and professional trajectories")

illustrate, we've taken a paragraph from Chapter 1 to show what different reading levels look like. Here's our original paragraph (1200–1300 Lexile level).

> Humans are naturally curious about how they compare to others. In a capitalistic society like the United States, ranking, scoring, and comparison are considered normal and generally expected. So, when we think about addressing and supporting adolescent literacy development, there is a push to conduct standardized and uniform ways to teach and assess learning.

Here's a revised version (600 Lexile level):

> People tend to wonder how they measure up to others. In America, a society that values competition and money, it's common to use rankings, scores, and comparisons to judge ourselves and others. This means that when we try to help young people become better readers and writers, we rely on tests and lessons that are the same for everyone. We want to make sure we're teaching and measuring things in a consistent way.

Many of the beginning teachers we've worked with are familiar, to some degree, with Lexile text measures. Lexile is one of the more popular calculations of quantitative text complexity measures and is the formula of choice for many schools. It's important to note that Lexile levels don't correspond with grade levels, so a range of them can be associated with a particular grade.

Knowing the quantitative measures of texts can help beginning teachers become more aware of what some students might struggle with when encountering a text. Secondary teachers can offer the same text at different reading levels to provide support for not-yet-proficient students. Many online resources such as Newsela, ReadWorks, Rewordify, News in Levels, and CommonLit provide texts for classroom use that are written at different text complexity levels.

A high school English Language Arts teacher we work with uses Orwell's (2021) essay "Politics and the English Language" in her classes during an informational text unit. She uses this essay to analyze Orwell's overall argument, the evidence for his argument, and the rhetorical strategies he uses. Because this teacher knows that some students are not-yet-proficient readers, they use an online tool to create several copies of this essay at different Lexile levels. In this way, students are exposed to the same content and can contribute to small-group and class discussions about Orwell's arguments.

Note that there are limitations to quantitative measures of text complexity because the content of the text is not considered when determining a complexity level. This becomes a limitation when texts have complex ideas but do not use complex language to express these ideas. For example, Elie Wiesel's *Night*, an autobiographical account of the author's survival as a teenager in the Nazi death camps, has a 590 Lexile level, which is connected with the complexity of texts at the 5th-grade level. However, while *Night* may not have complex language, it definitely has complex themes that are beyond the grasp of younger students, and this is why it is more generally used as a text in a 9th- or 10th-grade class where the average Lexile levels tend to be in the 1050–1335L range.

Quantitative measures of a text also need to be considered in terms of writing texts. Adolescents might have complex ideas but be unable to communicate them in writing. Perhaps their vocabulary knowledge is limited. In the case of many English Learners, they have complex ideas but are not yet able to express them in the English language or in writing. Whatever the case, it's important for secondary teachers to consider the writing complexities involved in particular writing assignments and activities. Online writing tools such as ChatGPT, Grammarly, and Hemingway Editor could be used to support English Learners in a variety of ways including brainstorming ideas, translating content, and making grammatical and mechanics choices.

Qualitative Measures of Print-Based Texts

Qualitative factors refer to how a text is organized and constructed. These can include the overall structure of a text, genre, text features, the background knowledge needed to understand the text, and the ways that language is used in the text. Qualitative factors are more difficult to measure because formulas can't measure these aspects of a text. Drawing on Fisher et al.'s (2012) work, the considerations listed in Table 4.3 can help determine the qualitative features of texts.

Text structures and genres refer to how fiction and nonfiction texts are organized and constructed in terms of content. A text can be organized in different forms such as medical charts, manuals, essays, and reports. Expository text structures include sequence/chronological order, classification, definition, process, description, comparison, problem/solution, and cause and effect. It's important to support students in understanding text structures because it allows them to better navigate their way through a text.

Text features are other aspects of text complexity. Text features are designed to help readers better understand the information. They can include a glossary, sidebar, diagrams, headings, table of contents, index, timeline, labels, charts, page numbers, titles, illustrations, subheadings, photographs, captions, bolded words, graphics, hyperlinks, and so on. Though each text feature has an objective, the overall purpose of text features is to help readers find information more easily.

Table 4.3. Qualitative Texts Measures of Print-Based Texts

Qualitative Text Measures	Considerations
Text Structure	Sequence/chronological order, classification, definition, process, description, comparison, problem/solution, or cause and effect
Text Genre	Familiar genre versus unfamiliar genre
Text Features	Text without features versus features that are meant to guide the reader, such as headings, subheadings, bolded words, graphics
Language Demands	Straightforward language versus figurative language such as imagery, metaphors, personification
Knowledge Demands	Few assumptions about readers' knowledge and experiences versus assuming knowledge about content, culture, etc.

Many times, we assume adolescents understand text structures, genres, and features, when in reality many adolescents overlook, underutilize, and misunderstand these aspects of texts. If we were to ask students to read a piece of sheet music, it might seem obvious that we would first check to make sure students understood musical notations and the purpose of visual symbols such as the bass and treble clefs. Making sure that adolescents understand the structures, genres, and features of other texts isn't that much different. When readers don't understand the purpose of text features and how they exist to support readers' comprehension, it makes sense to gloss over and ignore these features. Relatedly, when adolescents don't know how the main ideas and arguments are organized and supported in various texts, it's easy to get lost and miss some of the nuances and complexities and even the overall arguments themselves. When adolescent students can identify text features, structures, and genres, they are empowered to make sense of what they are reading and use this knowledge when they encounter texts independently.

Two other qualitative text measures contributing to a text's level of complexity include language and knowledge demands. Formal or academic language, for example, is much different from informal or conversational language, which sounds more like talking. Formal language has unique grammatical structures and ways of framing ideas, structuring arguments, and indicating relationships. These language demands can make a text harder to understand. Similarly, contemporary language is easier to read than the language used in the past. And, figurative language, as opposed to language written clearly and concisely, can be much harder to understand. Language demands in a text become particularly important to consider when supporting English Learners' literacy development.

> **COMPLEX LANGUAGE DEMANDS IN A HEALTH ARTICLE**
>
> Morris's (2022) *Wall Street Journal* article titled "What a Good Night's Sleep Can Do for Your Heart" has significant language demands that middle school health teachers should be aware of if they were to assign students to read this article. For example, the article uses technical vocabulary including "circadian rhythm" and "parasympathetic." There are several complex sentence structures with multiple clauses, such as, "In a study of nearly 4,000 middle-aged men and women, researchers found more atherosclerosis, a condition characterized by a buildup of fatty plaques in the arteries, in people who slept fewer than six hours a night than in those who got seven to eight hours." In addition, Morris presents nuanced ideas throughout the article that address sleep interruptions and sleep's effects on medical treatment. Highlighting these language and knowledge demands and sharing strategies for how to understand unknown words, complex sentence structures, and the development of the main ideas are all ways to support students' literacy skill development.

Knowledge demands refer to the kinds of experiences or knowledge expected of readers. If a text uses a lot of discipline-specific vocabulary, academic language, abstract nouns, and specialized terminology, the knowledge demands within this text are higher than if a text uses more informal and basic words and concepts. For example, if abstract nouns such as "freedom," "love," and "faith" are used or implied within a text, it might be harder for students to identify, define, and understand how these concepts are being used because they are abstract and thus more nuanced and complicated. In the same way, if a text includes references to specific historical events, scientific concepts, mathematical formulas, and literary devices, its knowledge demands are high. In contrast, texts that make no assumptions about readers' cultural, content, or disciplinary knowledge have easier knowledge demands and are less complex.

Reader and Task Considerations for Print-Based Texts

A final text complexity consideration is the "why" and "with whom" of using texts. In other words, we go beyond the text itself to consider the knowledge, abilities, and interests of the students who will be using the text as well as the instructional purposes for using the text. Collectively known as "reader and task considerations," this last category acknowledges that readers interact with texts differently because each reader comes with different skills, motivations, knowledge, and experiences. The RAND Reading Study Group (2002) offers helpful ways to think about reader and task considerations, shown in Table 4.4.

Identifying and Using Texts   71

For example, an economics teacher in a rural area of the United States struggles to find relevant and meaningful texts to engage her students, specific to their contexts and interests. For a unit on macroeconomics, the instructor chose Gillespie's (2018) article "How One Tiny Town is Battling 'Rural Brain Drain'" because the article explores the trend of young, educated people leaving rural areas for urban centers and the impact this migration has on rural economies. This was especially relevant to many of her students as they previously indicated their plans to move away after graduation. In addition to choosing this text, the teacher uses excepts from Vance's (2006) *Hillbilly Elegy* as well as current news articles highlighting the effects of weather or trade policies on crop prices, and the use of technology in farming. This teacher considers the "why" and "with whom" for the texts she chooses.

Considering the "why" and "with whom" of our use with particular texts can help us determine which texts to use with particular students for specific instructional purposes. It can also help us know when and how to differentiate texts among students. When we think about reader factors, we should consider students' reading skills, background knowledge, motivation, and engagement. As discussed in Chapter 2, different students have different experiences and skills with reading. Some might struggle with vocabulary words. Others might not read well because they aren't motivated to do so. In addition to this, our purposes for using the text are also important to consider—students might need to skim, scan, or do an in-depth reading of a text. As we'll discuss in the next section, there are many instructional purposes for using texts, and it's important to consider what skills students already have as well as what skills they might need to develop.

Non-Print-Based Texts

Many of the conversations around text complexity focus on print-based texts. Given our expanded definition of literacy to include more than just reading, it's also important to consider text complexity for visual, audio, verbal, spatial, gestural, and multimodal texts. What are ways to think about quantitative, qualitative, and reader and task considerations with timelines, microscopic photographs and graphs, short films, paintings or other artwork, and primary source artifacts? What kind of support might students need to have when using or creating these texts?

It's important to understand the different elements, structures, or features that contribute to the meaning-making or composition of non-print-based texts (Kist, 2013). Musical texts, for example, can draw on instrumentation, vocals, volume, tempo, rhythm, and message (lyrics). Films rely on sound design, camera angles and shots, movement, cinematography, and message. The structure of images includes lighting and color, placement, framing, use of symbols, and overall message (Krueger

Table 4.4. Reader and Task Considerations

Reader and Task Considerations	Question to Consider
Readers' Motivation and Interests	• Will students be interested in this text and motivated to read it? • Does this text connect to students' interests outside of school? • Might students feel confident and capable of reading this text?
Readers' Experiences	• Do students have previous experiences that might help them understand the text? • How might students' out-of-school experiences connect with the topics or themes in a text?
Readers' Knowledge of the Text Structures, Genre, and Language Used	• Do students have the needed vocabulary knowledge to understand this text? • Do they know enough about the topic? • Are students able to understand the language used (i.e., grammatical sentence structures, how different ideas connect with each other)? • Do students need support in understanding the text structure?
Readers' Knowledge of a Text's Ideas or Content	• Do students know what the text is about? Do they know the theme? • What do students know, in general, about the topic, theme, theory, or time period addressed in a text?
Readers' Skills	• What skills do students need to read this text? • Will they have the attention and memory to read it? What comprehension strategies will they need to rely on?
Purpose of Task(s)	• What kinds of literacy skills do students need to complete the task (i.e., making inferences, analyzing the author's craft, synthesizing information, evaluating arguments)? • How familiar are students with this purpose or task?

& Christel, 2001). Aspects of performances include acting, lighting and sound, costumes and make-up, sets, props, and overall message. For multimodal texts, it is consideration of all the elements in relationship to each other. With graphic novels, for example, we need to consider how both the visuals and the print text communicate the meaning of the story, at times in conflicting ways. Beyond understanding how the various elements work together in these different modes of texts, we also need to think about how these texts are complex and consider the maker's purpose, instructional

Identifying and Using Texts

Table 4.5. Qualitative Text Measures for Non-Print-Based Texts

Qualitative Text Measures	Considerations
Mode or Medium	What are the traditional conventions or characteristics of the mode or medium? Does the text conform to these expected conventions or characteristics?
Text Structure	How is the text organized and presented? What materials and techniques are used? What is the point of view? How are these features traditionally used?
Text Features	Is there supplemental information needed to understand the text?
Text Meaning and Purpose	What and how many levels of meaning and purpose are there in terms of symbolism?
Language Demands	What kind of language is used? Is it straightforward or figurative (i.e., using imagery, metaphors, personification)?
Knowledge Demands	What experiences or understandings are needed to make sense of the text?

purposes for using the text, as well as reader/viewer knowledge. To date, there are no quantitative measures or formulas to determine the readability of non-print texts. Cappello (2017) offers helpful categories that can be generally used and applied to non-print-based texts (Table 4.5).

Whatever non-print texts we use, we need to consider the instructional purposes of using these texts and the knowledge students might have (or not have) about both the kind of text it is and the content or meaning addressed in the text and the ways this meaning is communicated.

USING TEXTS FOR INSTRUCTIONAL PURPOSES

Texts can be used in a variety of ways across the subject areas to support instruction. Regardless of subject area, texts are used with students to introduce, practice, and review content. An obvious and familiar use of texts, in many subject areas, is to guide instruction in whole-class settings. Math textbooks, for example, determine the order and sequence of what is taught in math classrooms. Similarly, survey textbooks that cover a certain time period are used in history, English Language Arts, and world language classes and provide a curricular structure for lessons and units. In contrast, many art, physical education, and music classes don't use a central text to guide instruction, so teachers of these subject areas must find texts on their own.

However, texts can be used in a variety of creative ways to include and reference texts for instructional purposes. In some schools and districts, teachers have a lot of freedom in choosing texts to use in their classrooms. Other teachers, however, don't have the freedom to choose texts on their own because they've been handed a grade-wide or school curriculum from which they cannot deviate. Regardless of subject area and restrictions within the existing curriculum, the many ways to curate, use, and create texts with adolescents do have some flexibility. Even when teachers don't get to choose the texts in their curriculum, there are important ways to introduce, explain, and position all the texts we use.

One of the teachers we worked with taught a remedial high school English Language Arts class. In this course, the expectation that students would read "books at their level" presented multiple challenges, mainly related to students' lack of interest in texts they perceived to be "too young" and "childish." In concert with administrators and a collaborative colleague, this teacher revamped the course and added multiple texts beyond books. Students studied, analyzed, and discussed memes, YouTube videos, podcast episodes, children's literature, social media posts, websites, infographics, news articles, songs, short stories, and novels. This variety of texts afforded opportunities for students to expand their understanding of these modes and genres as well as to practice different literacy skills. At the same time, students remained engaged with complicated, nuanced topics relevant to their lived experiences and interests. As this teacher noted, this change increased students' motivation and stamina as they gained and practiced new literacy skills both with modes and genres they were familiar with and ones new to them.

This example illustrates Muhammad's (2020) concept of "layering texts." Muhammad describes "layering texts" as using "multiple short, powerful, multimodal texts" (p. 147) that support the mandated curriculum or textbook. Using texts in this way and in ways that support students' identity, skill, intellectual, and critical development can help students "understand local, national, and global communities and incite social critique" (p. 147). In this way, texts can introduce concepts or units of study and help deepen students' understanding of a topic by providing opportunities for synthesis and discussion. Texts can be used to access students' background knowledge or connect with their social media or popular culture use. Texts can also be used to highlight new vocabulary words, as examples of good writing about a topic, or as opportunities to analyze, evaluate, and synthesize information from multiple sources. Texts can help expose students to diverse perspectives and experiences.

In all of these instances, texts can be read aloud by the teacher to the class or watched or listened to collectively. Texts could also be assigned to small groups of students working together. Students could also read, listen to, or view texts independently in class or as homework. As the following example illustrates, teachers can make a variety of instruction choices with the texts they choose.

A beginning high school Spanish teacher we worked with utilized a six-box storyboard activity to support students' oral and written comprehension of a short story, a narrative text. The teacher gave each student a sheet of paper with six separate boxes, similar to a comic strip layout. Each box had one or two sentences at the bottom, written in Spanish. The instructor read the story aloud in Spanish, while simultaneously acting out parts and drawing images on the whiteboard as needed. As students listened, they drew what they heard and read. Afterward, they answered questions about the story on the backside of the worksheet. They wrote a new, amplified version of the story in Spanish, including different characters, locations, animals, and personalities.

To engage students in this activity, the instructor supported students' understanding of text structure, sequence, and genre (i.e., beginning, middle, and ending of a story). Additionally, the instructor explained the genre and structure of a storyboard—what it is and how it's organized (i.e., in boxes with in-text content and images, which readers read left to right and then top to bottom). In supporting students' understanding of multiple text structures, features, and genres, this instructor provided opportunities for students to consume and create a variety of Spanish texts.

Text Selection: Power and Privilege

As discussed in Chapter 3, literacy is not neutral, as some literacy contexts are privileged over others. It's important to consider the perspectives and experiences represented in texts. In our work with beginning teachers, we regularly reference Bishop's (1990a, 1990b) seminal argument that books can (and should) be windows and mirrors. Though Bishop uses this metaphor to discuss the importance of diverse representation in children's books, her metaphor has also been connected to multiple texts, topics, and subject areas at the secondary level (Frey, 2017; Sciurba, 2014).

Across subject areas, texts can act as mirrors to our experiences by reflecting back to us what we already relate to and/or identify with (e.g., race, gender, family structures, community norms). Other texts act as windows into or provide insight into experiences different from our own. These window texts offer insights and perspectives that are new or different. Students need to see themselves and their experiences in the texts they encounter, and they can learn much about the experiences of others in different texts (e.g., postsecondary pursuits, political beliefs, family structures, work experiences, religious affiliations, income levels, gender, sexual orientation, age, race/ethnicity, physical ability).

In a science class, texts could serve as windows and mirrors by exploring the contributions of diverse scientists and the impacts of science on different communities. A scientific article on the impact of climate change on Indigenous communities, for example, provides a window into the experiences of Indigenous people while also serving as a mirror for Indigenous students. In a math class, story problems can be used as window and mirror texts. Teachers can modify existing story problems or create their own to include names, identities, and situations of diverse individuals in their classrooms. For example, a story problem might involve calculating the amount of water needed for a community garden in a drought-prone region, highlighting the importance of water conservation. A geometry lesson might use examples of traditional and Indigenous architecture to illustrate geometric shapes and constructions. In a choir, orchestra, or band class, Asian, African, and Middle Eastern musicians and musical pieces may function as mirror texts to some students. Ensuring diversity of genres and musicians allows more students to see themselves in the music they learn and perform.

Connected to the texts used to support student learning, we encourage teachers to ask themselves questions about the texts they use (Table 4.6).

"YES, AND" APPROACH TO IDENTIFYING AND USING TEXTS

When we consider texts in a school context, it can be easy to think about only print-based texts. As noted earlier, a broader definition of text recognizes that, along with print based, texts can also be verbal, aural, spatial, gestural, and multimodal. As we consider situating our subject area content in ways that are relevant and meaningful to adolescent students, it's important to expand our ideas about texts beyond articles, books, and textbooks. Websites, podcasts, videos, TED talks, songs, and films, to name just a few, can be used across subject areas for instructional purposes. In this, a "yes, and" approach recognizes the value of traditional print-based texts and other textual modes.

A "yes, and" approach also recognizes adolescents' consumption and creation of texts outside school. Adolescents use texts in their homes, workplaces, places of worship, and other settings, and their interactions with these texts many times reveal their interests, identities, and expertise. When we recognize and build on these texts, we can increase engagement and motivation for learning in our subject areas. Further, when we know who our students are, what background knowledge they bring with them, what motivates them, and what literacy skills they have and might need, we can make better decisions about which texts to use and why.

Identifying and Using Texts

Table 4.6. Questions to Consider for Text Selection

Subject Area	Questions to Consider for Text Selection
English Language Arts	How are the authors of and characters and settings in my texts mirrors and windows for my students?
History	Whose perspective is foregrounded/backgrounded in the primary/secondary sources, images, and statistics included in my curriculum?
Math	Do students see themselves and their cultures, experiences, and communities represented in the examples and illustrations used in the texts, instruction, assignments, and assessments?
Science	Do students see themselves and their cultures, experiences, and communities represented in the scientists, discoveries, and research they study?
World Languages	Besides language acquisition, how are students taught to understand, explore, and appreciate cultural similarities and differences?
Health	Whose health matters? Are students' cultural/communal foods, diets, and health practices examined, celebrated, and incorporated in the curriculum?
Music	What music selections are students exposed to/expected to perform? Who wrote these? Where did they come from? What culture(s) and people do they reflect?
Art	Whose art is appreciated, valued, selected, studied, imitated? Why? Do students see themselves and their cultures, and communities represented in the artists, examples, and illustrations used in texts, instruction, assignments, and assessments?

MOVING FORWARD

In all subject areas, students need to encounter a wide range of materials, genres, and modes of texts in both volume and quantity. Ideally, students should interact with these texts for the same purposes as they do in the other contexts in their lives—information and pleasure. In addition, when possible, it's important for students to have choices in the texts they use in different subject areas based on interest and curiosity. Allowing students a choice of texts that are of high interest to them increases motivation, which can strengthen literacy skills. Teachers must also recognize students' experiences and expertise outside of the classroom. Adolescents consume and create texts independently, and many times these experiences and expertise are not recognized in classroom contexts. We need to identify these experiences and expertise, as well as adolescents' literacy skill development in using and creating school-based texts in the subject areas. In the next chapter, we'll explore ways to support students as they engage in these texts.

Questions to Consider

- *What texts do you currently use in your classroom? Why?*
- *What new texts might you include?*
- *How could you differentiate some of the texts you use?*

CHAPTER 5

Literacy Strategies Across Subject Areas

KEY TERMS

Content area literacy: a term used to describe the literacy strategies applicable to multiple subject areas

Literacy strategies: techniques or actions individuals use to improve their reading, writing, speaking, listening, and visual representation skills

In the previous chapter, we looked at identifying and selecting texts to use with adolescents across subject areas and considered the kinds of support adolescents might need as they encounter these texts, depending on their mode, genre, complexity level, and instructional purpose. In this chapter, we go further by focusing on strategies that can be used across subject areas to support adolescents' skill development as they interact with texts. To do this, we focus on two "yes, and" approaches, namely, that literacy instruction is the responsibility of all teachers and is multifaceted. As noted earlier, literacy refers to acquiring and using specific knowledge for particular purposes in a given context. This chapter focuses on how we acquire knowledge and how secondary teachers might better support their adolescent students as they read, write, listen, speak, view, and represent across the subject areas.

LITERACY SKILL DEVELOPMENT

Across the subject areas in middle and high school, adolescents encounter a broad range of complex texts. These texts have increasingly varied and more sophisticated structures, features, styles, and language and knowledge demands. To make sense of the musical scores, target language stories and articles, historical documents, podcasts, tables and figures, videos, websites, and reference materials, adolescents need to learn and apply new literacy skills. According to Fisher et al. (2016),

Literacy is a major engine in this [learning] process, as no matter how curious a child might be, his learning is limited by the constraints of his literacy skills. Therefore, we teach with intention, making sure that students acquire and consolidate the needed skills, processes, and metacognitive awareness that make self-directed learning possible." (p. 107)

Because of the increasingly complex texts in middle and high school, all students must learn and practice new skills and processes to support their learning. To become independent readers, writers, and thinkers, they need to be able to acquire and draw on a variety of literacy skills, processes, and strategies. Many of these are first introduced and used in elementary grades but then not reintroduced or reinforced at the secondary level because it's assumed that adolescent learners already know about and use many literacy strategies independently.

Although many terms are used in the field to describe ways to support students' literacy skills, we use "literacy strategy" to refer to teacher-directed techniques or approaches that support reading, writing, speaking, listening, viewing, and representing skills. Literacy strategies can help individuals develop the critical thinking skills they need to analyze, interpret, and create complex texts. These strategies can be used before, during, or after interacting with a text by both not-yet-proficient and proficient learners. For adolescent learners who are encountering increasingly complex texts across the subject areas, both familiar and new strategies can help them comprehend and produce longer and more content-focused texts and assignments.

As discussed in Chapter 2, some adolescents might struggle with literacy skills related to fluency, vocabulary, or comprehension. They might not have learned or remembered strategies that could help with these skills. Many times, English Learners need extra literacy support as they learn to acquire, use, and produce knowledge across the subject areas in a new language. They might know strategies to use in their home language but struggle to apply these strategies to texts written in English (Haas & Brown, 2019; Nora & Echevarria, 2016). Both of these groups of students need extra support in developing the needed skills and processes to become independently proficient readers, writers, speakers, and thinkers.

Other adolescents learned literacy strategies when they were younger but do not yet use these strategies independently or know them well enough to be able to apply them to new texts. For example, many students inherently understand the importance of previewing a text and do so without thinking. When they read an article, they notice the length and look at the title to determine what the article is about. But, at times, it can be harder for them to know how and why to use this previewing strategy when encountering a new or complex text. When adolescents read a research article about the benefits of exercise, they may need to be reminded that the article title, section headings, and paragraph structures give guideposts for determining the main ideas and overall argument. While most secondary teachers are not trained reading coaches or interventionists, they can nonetheless support their students' literacy skill development through the use of literary strategies.

Identifying Literacy Skills

Many beginning teachers have a hard time initially identifying the literacy strategies, skills, processes, and metacognitive awareness they regularly use or that they could work on with students. This is because many of the literacy skills we have acquired over the years have become automatic and internal. We forget what it's like to learn content or encounter certain kinds of texts for the first time. As proficient learners, we regularly draw on and use literacy skills across different contexts and don't even realize it. For example, if we read something we don't understand, many of us automatically re-read the sentence or paragraph. In our re-reading, we might pause if we encounter a word we don't know and then rely on context clues to determine its meaning. Our re-reading might also involve overlooking a word we don't know but focusing instead on the main ideas in a paragraph or section to make sense of the passage.

Proficient readers use strategies when encountering texts. For example, they visualize, notice, and connect with background knowledge, monitor their thinking, determine importance, infer, make predictions, and preview texts. In addition, they know what to do when they get stuck or confused (Table 5.1).

When secondary teachers work together across subject areas to identify and integrate these generic literacy skills, adolescent students have more opportunities to learn about, acquire, and practice these skills. This matters because adolescents' literacy development benefits when they can apply similar strategies across courses and content. The more they do this, the better they can internalize these strategies and use them independently. Going back to the re-reading example from above, when adolescents learn, practice, and apply a re-reading strategy, the more it becomes part of what they automatically do when encountering a text or what they could decide to do when they struggle to understand a text.

Some schools identify particular strategies to focus on across subject areas and even encourage (or require) teachers to hang up posters that list these strategies. We appreciate this schoolwide approach because literacy support needs to go beyond an individual teacher's classroom walls. The following case study illustrates how this collaborative approach might work.

Table 5.1. Successful Interactions With a Text

Reading Strategy	Examples
Activate Prior Knowledge	Use previous knowledge to make connections and understand new information
Monitor Comprehension	Check for understanding during reading and adjust reading strategies as needed
Summarize Main Ideas	Identify main ideas and restate in own words
Make Inferences	Use information to make educated guesses about what might happen next or what the author is trying to communicate
Ask Questions	Ask questions during reading to deepen understanding of the text
Use Context Clues	Use surrounding words and sentences to figure out meaning of unfamiliar words or ideas
Make Predictions	Make predictions during reading to monitor comprehension, form hypotheses, stay engaged
Visualize Information	Visualize ideas and information to deepen comprehension and engagement

Schoolwide Strategy Implementation: Re-Reading

At the beginning of the school year, a high school principal shared with her teachers that the goal for the year was to increase students' literacy skills. To support her teachers with this goal, the district's curriculum director led a professional development day for all high school teachers. During this time of learning, the curriculum director identified five literacy strategies she wanted all teachers across 9th–12th grades to teach and model throughout the school year. One of these five strategies was re-reading. The curriculum director encouraged teachers to first explain re-reading to their students, then to model re-reading passages of texts they assigned or used in class, and, finally, to provide ongoing opportunities in class for students to re-read texts. Students were encouraged to use re-reading when they did not fully understand something they read. Moreover, students were expected to use re-reading with a variety of texts, including scores of music in band and choir, artists' statements and machine manuals in art and industrial education, graphs and charts in social studies and math, articles about sexual health and humans' brain function in health and psychology, as well as poems, narratives, and novels in English and world languages. The larger goal was that through intentionally integrating, modeling, and expecting re-reading to occur across their school day, students would then also use re-reading to support their comprehension and understanding of out-of-school texts, such as directions, menus, text messages, instruction manuals, job applications, and tax forms.

USING LITERACY STRATEGIES TO SUPPORT ADOLESCENTS' LITERACY SKILL DEVELOPMENT

The purpose of using literacy strategies like re-reading is to support students' skill development by helping them learn how, when, and why to use them on their own. When teachers in any subject area purposefully and intentionally introduce and practice literacy strategies for instructional purposes, students learn to use strategies when interacting with texts, either in classroom settings or on their own. Realizing that not all strategies will work with the same effectiveness for every learner or with every subject matter, learning goal, or text, it's important to introduce and have students know and practice as many strategies as possible. Strategies contribute to overall literacy skills and help us know what to do when we get stuck or confused with a text.

Literacy strategies include a wide range of techniques, from basic reading comprehension strategies like summarizing and predicting to more advanced techniques like analyzing text structure and making connections between different texts. As we'll see later in the chapter, strategies can be used before, during, or after encountering a text. Furthermore, some strategies are more specific to reading, listening to, and/or viewing a text (e.g., pre-reading, monitoring comprehension). In contrast, others are more applicable when writing and revising a text (e.g., drafting, outlining, revising). We've found it helpful to think about literacy strategies based on the particular aspect of literacy they typically focus on (e.g., comprehension, vocabulary, writing, discussion, and visually representing). Additional aspects can be associated with strategies depending on how they are used within a particular context, as shown in Table 5.2. For example, the use of the KWL (Know, Want to Know, Learned) chart strategy could include visual representation (i.e., students draw what they learned) or discussion (i.e., students discuss what they want to learn in pairs, small groups, or as a class).

Conversations about literacy strategies have a long, rich history in the field of adolescent literacy, which started in the early 20th century. Referred to today as "content area literacy," this body of scholarship focuses on supporting students' generic literacy skills in school settings for academic purposes. Researchers in this area look at what proficient readers and writers do across all content areas. Researchers then identify how to explicitly teach these strategies, techniques, methods, and skills to those who are not yet proficient.

Table 5.2. Selected Literacy Strategy Focus

Selected Literacy Strategy	Comprehension	Visually representing	Vocabulary	Writing	Speaking
Concept Map: Visually represent relationships and connections between ideas	X	X		X	
RAFT: Helps students structure writing about a text by considering Role, Audience, Format, and Topic	X			X	
List Group Label: Organizing thoughts and categorizing information	X		X		X
Predicting: Using prior knowledge, context clues, and text features to anticipate what will happen next	X	X		X	X
Paragraph Shrinking: Condensing a paragraph into a shorter summary	X			X	
KWL (Know, Want to Know, Learned) Chart	X		X	X	

Systems of education and educators' pedagogies and practices are situated in multiple historical and cultural contexts. Historically, conversations around literacy strategies focused solely on reading. As understandings of literacy broadened over time, the field of literacy education expanded to include writing, speaking, and visually representing strategies. This historical perspective of the field is important because it explains some of the current emphasis on reading strategies that remain as well as some of the resistance to the idea that "every teacher is a reading teacher" (Beers, 2003; Draper, 2002). By historically focusing on reading and by reading particular kinds of print-based texts, the "content area literacy" movement has, at times, perpetuated a narrow definition of literacy (i.e., literacy is reading), including the idea that literacy is generic and the same across contexts. As we'll see in Chapter 6, knowledge is acquired in particular ways for specific purposes in specific contexts. Thus, supporting literacy skills, while necessary and needed, must recognize the different ways knowledge is acquired, used, and produced across the subject areas.

Reading Strategies

Reading strategies support students' understanding of written texts and are sometimes referred to as "comprehension strategies." These strategies focus on helping students monitor or become aware of their understanding and when they might get stuck or confused. Reading strategies can focus on helping students find and figure out inferences, summarize texts, and activate background knowledge. To illustrate, a high school French teacher we've worked with uses a reading comprehension strategy called "skim and scan" to support students' reading comprehension. At the beginning of each unit, the instructor invites students to scan and, when applicable, skim content as they examine the unit's headings, subheadings, and graphics in the textbook. This strategy enables adolescents to understand what they will be learning. This strategy also helps students build schema and connect new information to background knowledge. Strategies such as Directed Reading Thinking Activity, Jigsaw, Question–Answer Relationship, and Double-Entry Journal can be used to make predictions, ask questions, notice vocabulary words, and articulate understanding of a text (Table 5.3). These and other reading strategies offer students various plans of action that help students gain independence as proficient readers across texts and genres.

Reading Strategies: English Language Arts

Over the years, Erica and her preservice teachers have engaged in various book club experiences with a 6th-grade teacher, Ms. Saffron, and her

Table 5.3. Reading Strategy Suggestions

Reading Strategy	Description	Before, During, or After Reading
Directed Reading Thinking Activity	Students make predictions, ask questions, and then read to confirm, disprove, or respond to their predictions or questions	Before, During, or After
Jigsaw	Students are assigned to reading groups. Each group member is assigned one section of the text and is responsible for becoming an "expert" on it and then teaching it to the other group members	After
Question–Answer Relationship	Students are given four kinds of questions to look for in a text, as well as the answers to the questions, which include Right There Questions; Think and Search Questions; Author and You Questions; On My Own Questions	After
Double-Entry Journal	In a two-column table, students write down vocabulary words, phrases, or sentences from the reading on one side and their reactions to the chosen text excerpts on the other	During

students, where preservice teachers facilitated weekly conversations and activities with small groups of 6th-graders connected to a specific text. One semester, the selected text was Paul Fleischman's (2013) novella *Seedfolks*. Another semester they collectively read and discussed Linda Sue Park's (2010) story about one of the "Lost Boys" of Sudan, as told in *A Long Walk to Water*. These book club experiences have also included William Alexander's (2013) dystopian fantasy *Goblin Secrets* and Jacqueline Woodson's (2015) novel *Locomotion*, a story about siblings in foster care.

One assumption about this school–university book club partnership was that the 6th-graders could independently decode each text. In other words, when working with a hard copy of the novel, it was expected that these adolescents would be able to recognize and read the words, paragraphs, and chapters of the selected text. As a result, 6th-graders were expected to read portions before they met with Erica's undergraduate students in their small groups. This meant that the instructional focus in these book club groups centered on supporting adolescents' literacy development with a specific emphasis on the 6th-graders' comprehension of the text.

To support their reading development when studying Alexander's *Goblin Secrets* (2012), Ms. Saffron wanted her 6th-grade students to discuss the text within their small-group book clubs led by preservice teachers. To support her students' literacy development, Ms. Saffron provided students with reading strategies that they and the preservice teachers would use when they met, including the following:

- Ask questions to clarify understanding.
- Give a reason to support an idea.
- Ask for evidence when something sounds inaccurate or vague.
- Give evidence to support statements.
- Use ideas from others to add to their own.

Vocabulary Strategies

An overlooked aspect of reading comprehension is vocabulary knowledge and strategies around what to do when encountering an unfamiliar word. Beck et al.'s (2013) tiered model of vocabulary words helps to identify words for students to learn. Tier 1 words are words that most people know, such as "talk," "argue," "watch," and "respond." Tier 2 words are academic words used across subject areas, such as "matrix," "analysis," "evidence," "cause," and "effect." Tier 3 words refer to discipline-specific and technical words, such as "slope," "onomatopoeia," "fascist," and "crescendo." In thinking about vocabulary support, it's important to explicitly teach Tier 2 words by using vocabulary strategies and learning vocabulary words in context.

Rather than memorizing vocabulary words and making lists of words, a variety of effective vocabulary strategies can be used instead. These include using graphic organizers such as word maps. A word map is a template-based visual representation students complete to help them learn definitions and uses of given words. In addition to the vocabulary term, word maps generally include blank spaces for students to write the word's definition as well as synonyms and antonyms, along with a sentence in which they demonstrate their ability to understand and use the word correctly. Word maps can also help students visualize and categorize new vocabulary words and help them understand the relationship between words and their meanings. Word games like crossword puzzles, word scrambles, and word searches can also be used to help students practice and reinforce new vocabulary words. A classroom "word wall" is another vocabulary strategy that can support students' vocabulary development by helping them see and use new words in context.

Vocabulary Strategies: Math

In a pre-calculus class, students have been struggling to remember the meaning of key vocabulary. The teacher decides to use a vocabulary strategy, namely, a graphic organizer (i.e., Frayer model), to help students understand terms such as "function," "domain," and "range." The graphic organizer includes sections for the term being defined, its definition, examples, and non-examples. After making copies of the graphic organizer, the instructor asked students to fill out the sections for "function." When the graphic organizer was complete, students utilized their work as a reference to remind them of the selected terms.

In their Algebra 1 class, the same instructor used another vocabulary strategy: word maps. A word map includes the term being defined, its definition, synonyms, antonyms, and a visual representation. After the teacher explained and modeled the strategy, students added to their word map and were encouraged to use this resource as a study guide before assessments.

Writing Strategies

Many of the beginning teachers we work with underutilize writing strategies in their classrooms because they envision writing as either short answers to factual questions on tests, creative writing, or long, end-of-the-unit papers. Writing, however, can be regularly used to help deepen students' understanding of what they've learned, to support their ability to communicate ideas, and to support their writing skills. "Writing to learn" strategies help students organize their thoughts, clarify main ideas, and remember what they have learned. This can be done through written conversations between students and exit slips (Daniels & Zemelman, 2014).

Note-taking strategies such as the Cornell Method can support students in recording and reviewing notes. With this strategy, students divide a note-taking page into three columns that leave room for main ideas, notes, and a summary of the main ideas. Strategies such as Quickwrites (Daniels & Zemelman, 2014) can also be used to help students practice their writing fluency. These short, timed writing activities allow students to generate ideas and explore their thoughts. Students can also be empowered in their own writing and their reading by learning how paragraphs and sentences are put together and how different writing genres and purposes require different rhetorical approaches.

General writing strategies can support both transcription and composing writing skills. These general writing strategies include examining mentor texts (i.e., examples or models), generating outlines and/or drafts before writing, reading one's own writing aloud to identify and correct errors, using a peer-review process to support students' writing development, and employing formula-based writing (e.g., five-paragraph essays) to assist students' ability to structure and organize their ideas.

Writing Strategies: History and Health

At the beginning of the school year, Ms. Abdullah's 9th-grade U.S. history class studied a unit focused on the American Civil War, including its causes and effects. To assess students' understanding after this unit, Ms. Abdullah assigned a five-paragraph essay assignment centered on the impact of the cause–effects connected to this war, as listed in the assignment description. To support their learning, Ms. Abdullah reminded her students about the importance of brainstorming and modeled brainstorming as a writing strategy. She used a classroom whiteboard and dry-erase markers to write down her ideas as she talked aloud. She explained her thinking, generating a list of ideas and then putting them into a five-paragraph essay outline template to organize ideas. Once she had a brainstorm generated on the whiteboard, she asked her students to select one of the U.S. Civil War causes and effects and create their own brainstorming lists. First, they captured their ideas using paper and pencils already at their desks. Then they used the same five-paragraph essay outline template Ms. Abdullah provided to determine organizational structures for their essays.

Following this modeling and instruction, students were asked to create and turn in their initial brainstorming and essay outline drafts, which Ms. Abdullah reviewed. Once she reviewed her students' work, she reviewed the structure of a five-paragraph essay (i.e., an introductory paragraph, three body paragraphs, and a conclusion paragraph). To support her students' learning, Ms. Abdullah handed out copies of two anonymized five-paragraph essays from former students. Reading these examples aloud, she asked students to (1) label the parts of the essay, (2) underline both the thesis and restated thesis, and (3) highlight supporting examples in each body paragraph. This activity was intended to ensure that Ms. Abdullah's students understood the five-paragraph essay format and the expectations for the cause–effect writing assignment they would complete and turn in.

Concurrently, many of Ms. Abdullah's 9th-grade U.S. history students also had Mr. Singh for health. While they were studying the American Civil War and working on a five-paragraph cause–effect writing assignment in Ms. Abdullah's class, Mr. Singh's 9th-grade health students were learning about the benefits of cardio exercise. Throughout the unit, as they read and learned about cardio, Mr. Singh and his students captured the benefits on a graphic organizer handout. To assess their understanding of this content at the end of the unit, Mr. Singh asked students to use a free online tool to create a one-page infographic highlighting the benefits of cardio exercise.

When introducing this assignment, Mr. Singh first asked students to review the content on their graphic organizer. Then he explained that when beginning a new writing assignment, brainstorming was a strategy that students could use to capture initial ideas and help them begin to think about what they wanted to write about. He then directed them to highlight the three benefits they thought were most important. Students worked in small groups to discuss their ideas, with the invitation to change or adjust their thinking after listening to their peers. Mr. Singh then reviewed the writing assignment. He shared some sample infographics related to other health topics and reminded students about the components of an effective infographic, including minimal text and clear images. These infographics would be posted around the school to encourage students to use cardio exercises to stay healthy. He assigned a due date for a draft with the expectation that students would share their infographic drafts during an in-class peer-review process before turning in their final drafts.

Discussion Strategies

Research shows that when students interact with each other around texts, their understanding increases (Frey et al., 2008). Given this, it can be easy to assume that students know how to have a "discussion" with partners, in small groups, or as a whole class. But research also shows that for student talk to be effective, explicit speaking or discussion skills need to be taught and modeled (Nystrand, 2006). However, we've found, and the research points to it, that students need explicit training before, during, and after conversations with peers (Daniels & Steienke, 2011). In addition, having conversations about the texts we read, write, listen to, or view is important.

The simple and quick "Talk and Turn" or "Think-Pair-Share" discussion strategies are some of our favorites to use. Both strategies utilize a prompt from a teacher, inviting students to consider a question, idea, or statement. With "Talk and Turn," students discuss responses to the prompt with a peer located near or next to them. Similarly, with "Think-Pair-Share" activities, students first think about the prompt and then pair up with a partner (pre-assigned or based on proximity). Then, after students discuss their responses to the prompt with one or more partners, they share a written or verbal summary of the conversation to demonstrate their understanding and learning. These can be extended into larger discussion strategies such as the Socratic Seminar, which involves students talking about a text in a small group guided by open-ended questions from a facilitator to promote critical thinking, active listening, and respectful debate.

Talk stems are another discussion strategy to use across subject areas to support students' speaking skills. Talk stems are short sentence-starters that provide students with prompts for participating in peer-to-peer and class discussions. They can be used to help students share their ideas, ask questions, and build on each other's thinking. Returning to our earlier example of the partnership between Erica's preservice teachers and local middle school students, Ms. Saffron knew that although her 6th-graders enjoyed talking and listening to their peers, they weren't yet skilled with text-based discussions. To support adolescents' speaking and listening development in this area, Ms. Saffron utilized talk stems, a discussion strategy employed to support students' speaking, listening, and writing skills. Specific talk stems were provided to each student and preservice teacher (Table 5.4).

Table 5.4. Selected Talk Stems

Discussion Purpose	Possible Talk Stems
Talking About Author's Purpose/Message	The author's purpose for writing is . . . The author wrote this because . . . The big idea in this text is . . . The author's message is . . .
Analyzing Author's Credibility	The author provides support by . . . The author is best qualified to write about . . . The author is making the assumption that . . . The author used . . . to support their ideas about . . .
Clarifying Understanding of Text	Can you tell me more about . . . Would you say that again, please? What makes you say that? This reminds me of . . . because I think . . . is true.
Sharing Textual Evidence to Support Claims	Can you show me a place in the text that supports your idea? It says here [read passage/section], which explains/relates to . . .
Considering Points of View	When I read . . . I can see what the author thinks because . . . This text suggests that the author's opinion about . . . is . . . A point of view missing from this text is . . . because . . .
Asking for Clarifications	Can you tell me more about . . . ? Can you give me an example of what you mean? This reminds me of . . . because . . . I think this is true because . . . I'm not sure about this. Can you tell me why you think this is true?

Each week, students highlighted a new talk stem on their handout that they would intentionally use during their book club discussion. Each small group consisted of three to five students and one preservice teacher. In each group, students first shared the prompt they planned to use. Then the preservice teacher in that group read aloud the discussion questions Ms. Saffron provided, inviting students to verbally respond with their thinking, listen to and build on their peers' responses, and point to evidence in the text to support or challenge their own and peers' responses. At the end of the discussion, students offered feedback about their group's conversation, including which talk stems seemed to work well and why.

After reading the novel, students were required to generate a written response connected to the book. One of the expectations of this written response was that students would include at least three of the talk stems from the handout they used to frame their ideas and support their claims. Given their versatility and applicability across subject areas, talk stems are an effective discussion strategy, and the intention was that Ms. Saffron's 6th-grade students could and would use these talk stems in their other classes to further develop literacy skills, particularly those associated with speaking, listening, and writing.

Visual Strategies

Visual strategies refer to the techniques and skills used to interpret and communicate meaning through visual images such as photographs, illustrations, charts, diagrams, and videos. Given that visual information is prevalent and used in many forms of media, supporting students' development of these strategies is important. A "Mind Mapping" strategy, for example, involves creating a visual diagram of the main topic or concept and its related subtopics or details. This strategy, along with others such as graphic organizers, flow charts, Venn diagrams, and concept maps, encourage students to connect and organize information in a nonlinear way and to see relationships between ideas and concepts.

In using these visual literacy strategies, individuals can enhance their ability to communicate, collaborate, and understand visual information in a more meaningful and effective way. In addition, different strategies and skills are associated with digital literacy. When we read digital texts, for example, it can be easier to skim and read faster, so it might be helpful to use digital annotation tools or speed-reading apps to help eliminate distractions (Salmerón & Llorens, 2019; Turner & Hicks, 2015). In other words, we need to use new strategies and develop different skills to be proficient learners in digital and multimodal contexts. For example, writing now includes activities such as generating multimodal social media posts (text and images/videos), creating websites, and coding. While all of these literacy practices involve writing, they require different tools and approaches, not to mention different audiences and purposes than those of the past.

USING LITERACY STRATEGIES FOR INSTRUCTIONAL PURPOSES

Given all the potential literacy strategies available, it's important to consider what, when, and how a particular strategy might be used. Literacy strategies can be taught and practiced individually, in small groups and in whole-group settings. They can also be used at different times throughout a lesson, series of lessons, or unit (Table 5.5).

Identifying which skill or outcome is needed is the first step in determining which strategies to use with students. Once the outcome(s) is (are) identified, teachers should then identify which strategies will be most

Table 5.5. Using Literacy Strategies Before, During, and After Encountering Texts

Literacy Strategy	Before	During	After
Activate Prior Knowledge	X		
Anticipation Guides	X		
Context Clues		X	
Entrance Tickets	X		
Evaluate Understanding			X
Exit Slips			X
KWL (Know, What to Know, Learned) Charts	X	X	X
Make Inferences		X	X
Make Predictions	X	X	
Monitor Comprehension		X	
Note-Taking		X	
Questioning the Author/Speaker			X
Pre-Read or Preview a text	X		
Re-Read		X	X
Set Goal(s) and Establish Purpose	X		
Summarize		X	X
Text Structures		X	
Think-Alouds	X	X	X
Vocabulary Sorts	X		
Word Wall	X	X	

helpful for students' learning. Intentionally aligning strategies with intended outcomes more likely ensures that the strategies used will support students' learning (Wiggins & McTighe, 2005). For example, Mr. Fola, a high school health teacher, identifies National Health Education Standard 2.12.1: "Analyze how the family influences the health of individuals" (Joint Committee on National Health Education Standards, 2007) as an upcoming unit outcome. He selects the vocabulary strategy Word Wall as a means to support his students' learning. The purpose of a word wall is to provide a visual reference of identified vocabulary words, making words accessible and visible. Mr. Fola chooses this strategy because he wants students to understand, become familiar with, and be able to use words such as alcoholism, genetics, hypertension, immunizations, socioeconomic status, and food insecurity. He also wants his students to start seeing themes, categories, and connections between these words.

After choosing a strategy, it's important to explicitly introduce, model, and explain the whats, whys, and hows of the strategy to students as well as to provide multiple opportunities for practice and application. It's important to explain the purpose of the strategy and its connection to larger literacy skills because strategies should always be used to help students better understand course content or learn to navigate a text. Strategies should be used to support students in developing skills that they can eventually internalize. Strategies should be used to foster students' comprehension and capacity to communicate their learning while also developing their independence when encountering and producing texts on their own.

A "gradual release framework" of instruction, made popular by Pearson and Gallagher (1983) provides a helpful way to think about using literacy strategies with students. This instructional approach involves explicit strategy instruction that includes the following steps: identifying the strategy, explaining it, modeling it, and then giving students time to practice it. Throughout the gradual release model, the teacher gradually releases responsibility to the students, starting with more support and scaffolding and moving toward more independent practice. When using strategies in the classroom, it's important for teachers to model the use of the strategy to students while also explaining what the strategy is and how to use it. Then, teachers should have students practice the strategy on their own and check in to see how they are doing with it.

Returning to the health class example, Mr. Fola shares with his students both digital and classroom examples of health-related Word Walls. He describes the purpose of the strategy and then tells students how they will be contributing to and using a Word Wall during the unit. Mr. Fola distributes a handout to students that contains a chart with columns for words, definitions, and images. He uses several vocabulary words from a previous unit to model for students how to use the chart and how to start thinking about connections, themes, and categories of the selected words.

He invites students to keep track of words they encounter throughout the unit that might describe how families influence the health of individuals. As the unit progresses, he creates intentional opportunities for students to complete and post word wall entries. He invites them to refer to the word wall during class or small-group discussions.

* * *

Literacy strategies can also be used for formative assessment purposes and can give teachers access to students' thinking. Below are some of our favorite literacy strategies to use in this way.

- **Exit tickets:** An exit ticket is a short written response that students complete at the end of a lesson or class period. For learners, an exit ticket provides an opportunity to synthesize information and monitor comprehension. It can also provide teachers insight into areas where students may need additional support or clarification.
- **Close reading:** Close reading is a reading strategy that involves careful analysis of a text. Teaching students how to do a close reading involves asking them to read a passage and then annotate the text by highlighting key terms, circling unfamiliar words, and underlining important ideas. Teachers could use these annotations to determine how well students are understanding a text.
- **Think-Pair-Share:** This cooperative discussion strategy involves individual reflection, small-group discussion, and whole-class sharing. Teachers could use the class discussion as a formative assessment tool to determine how well students are understanding the concepts and ideas in a lesson.
- **Graphic organizers:** Graphic organizers, such as Venn diagrams, help students organize and categorize information. They can be particularly useful in comparing and contrasting ideas or information. Teachers can use students' completed graphic organizers to gauge how well students understand similarities and differences between ideas.

Across all of these instructional purposes for using strategies, it's important that literacy strategies should always be a means to a greater end. In other words, don't make the strategies themselves the focus. This might be easier said than done, particularly when introducing students to a new strategy. At times, to teach a strategy well, the end goal or outcome of the strategy isn't addressed and too much time is spent on the strategy itself. The overall goal of all strategies should be increased automaticity and self-regulation, and, according to some researchers, strategies can be learned quickly and don't require much practice (Willingham &

Lovette, 2014). In addition, the purpose should be to support subject area knowledge.

Be aware that some strategies are more effective than others. Much research is associated with analyzing the effectiveness of strategies in supporting students' learning. For example, Hattie's (2008) meta-analysis of empirical studies identified positive effects related to student learning outcomes connected to particular factors, strategies, and interventions used to support students' learning. In a follow-up study, Hattie and Yates's (2013) connected the outcomes from these meta-analyses with cognitive psychology and the "science of learning," centering humans' developmental and cognitive needs and characteristics at the center of the learning process. Drawing on Hattie's (2008) work, Fisher et al. (2016) note several specific strategies and approaches teachers can use to support students' K–12 literacy development. This type of research has been used in many educational settings to identify "what works" connected to strategies used to support teaching and learning.

"YES, AND" APPROACH TO USING LITERACY STRATEGIES ACROSS SUBJECT AREAS

A "yes, and" approach recognizes that literacy skill development is needed in middle and high school. Literacy strategies need to be explicitly taught and practiced across subject areas to support adolescents' literacy development. When it comes to adolescent literacy, reading and writing strategies are foregrounded and prioritized. We understand why this happens, particularly with the pressures of standardized testing and the need for students' reading and writing scores to measure as proficient. However, it's important to remember that adolescents need support in developing other literacy skills as well. Videos, podcasts, web-based memes and gifs, interactive websites, augmented reality, and social media are now also part of the curriculum and part of adolescents' experiences out of school. Remembering to support our students' learning with strategies for encountering these multimodal texts is also important. Speaking and listening during a class discussion or in-class presentation; visually representing ideas in a Science class; creating graphs, tables, and images; and learning how to perform a piece of music or an athletic skill related to a particular sport are also important.

With the increase of digital technologies and multimedia texts and the broadening of understandings of literacy to include more than just print-based text, conversations about literacy strategies now encompass more than just reading and writing to include speaking, listening, visually representing, and viewing skills. Adolescents need *literacy* strategies, which include strategies that support learners' abilities to listen, speak, perform, and represent their learning, rather than just reading and/or writing strategies.

MOVING FORWARD

Teachers of all subject areas can support their adolescent students' literacy development through the use of strategies. There is much to gain when secondary teachers use these strategies with their students, not only in their own classrooms but also in collaboration with colleagues across subject areas. Particularly when implemented consistently over time and across grade levels and subject areas at the secondary level, the use of literacy strategies allows adolescents to practice applying and using these strategies with the texts they encounter and produce. Long-term, these strategies can become part of adolescents' learning repertoires and support their independence and growth so they have tools and skills to use to learn and communicate their learning.

Questions to Consider

- *What literacy-related skills do your students need to further develop?*
- *Which literacy strategies work well in your subject area(s)?*
- *How might you partner with colleagues to increase students' opportunities to practice and develop certain literacy strategies and their associated skills?*

CHAPTER 6

Disciplinary Literacy Instruction

KEY TERMS

Disciplinary literacy: the different ways professionals within the disciplines acquire, use, and produce knowledge

Disciplinary literacy instruction: instructional methods that align closely with the profession(s) and communities associated with each discipline

In our last chapter, we explored ways to support adolescent learners across subject areas as they develop their literacy skills in school. Literacy strategies help adolescents acquire and use knowledge as they read, write, speak, listen, and represent across subject areas. In this chapter, we extend the conversation to explore how literacy instruction can support specific purposes within specific disciplines. We focus on a "yes, and" approach to commonly held literacy beliefs, namely, that literacy refers to general and specific skills and that literacy instruction needs to be contextual, with skill development aligning with the practices of different disciplines. General literacy skills can work across all subject areas, but specific ways of reading, writing, speaking, listening, and representing are also unique to each subject area.

DISCIPLINARY LITERACY

Disciplinary literacy is a term that describes how professionals in different disciplines acquire, use, evaluate, and produce knowledge. Within each discipline, its members are trained to think about, see, and even move in the world in specific ways (Wickens et al., 2015). Members also use knowledge, tools, and skills to access, organize, communicate, create, and assess the information within that discipline as well as to ask questions that reflect these ways of seeing, knowing, and thinking (O'Brien et al., 1995; Shanahan & Shanahan, 2012; Wineburg, 2001; Wineburg et al., 2013). The ways in which people in different disciplines read and write, the questions they ask, the details they notice, and how they produce knowledge or critique existing knowledge are thus particular or specialized given their disciplinary contexts. Further, different kinds of texts are read and written for different purposes, so literacy is different within each discipline. For example, science classes focus on the processes observable in nature and use inquiry-based ways to test new theories. English and history classes consider human constructs and concerns and, using humanities-based methods, construct and support arguments. Musicians and artists use creative expression to create and interpret the arts. However, it is more than just content that distinguishes the disciplines. There are differences in how content is consumed and created because disciplines represent cultures that use language differently and have their own ways of reading, writing, speaking, and thinking.

We've likely seen and even heard evidence of disciplinary literacy when we've talked with various professionals about their work. A builder, for example, when describing a residential remodeling project they're engaged in, will use different terms and tools to describe and complete their work than does a lawyer who serves as a guardian ad litem for children in foster care. The work of a builder and lawyer varies, including the terminology and approaches they use and how these professionals think through, navigate, and understand the systems in which they work and address problems. In terms of academic disciplines, historians contextualize what they read by thinking about past events and perspectives. Scientists, on the other hand, approach their work by studying phenomena and predicting what might happen in the future.

The following questions help identify the key components of what it means to be literate within a discipline:

- What do experts or insiders in a particular field of study do?
- What are the goals and practices of each discipline?
- How do learning standards work toward this?
- How might particular classroom activities be described or explained in ways that connect with the real work of the discipline?

Disciplinary Literacy in Action: English Language Arts and Social Studies

When helping beginning teachers understand disciplinary literacy, we share a video featuring a high school English Language Arts teacher and a high school social studies teacher who employ disciplinary literacy approaches to a common text (Disciplinary Literacy for Deeper Learning MOOC-Ed, 2014). In this video, each teacher uses the literacy strategy of close reading to examine and consider a common text, "The Gettysburg Address," a speech delivered by President Abraham Lincoln on November 19, 1863, four and a half months after the Union's victory on this battlefield. Although each teacher uses the same literacy strategy and examines the same text, they notice different things about it and ask separate questions. Taking on the role of a literary critic, the English Language Arts teacher first notes how figurative language, such as the initial metaphors in Lincoln's speech, frames this speech. For example, the speaker focused on the broader idea related to the birth of a nation and utilized "conception-oriented" language to connote a new birth arising from this particular battle. Moreover, the shift in tense within the speech is a rhetorical move the speaker uses to juxtapose the nation's beginning and the battle that took place earlier on this site with the present day.

In contrast, the social studies teacher who reads the text as a historian first notes the document's historical context, particularly that Lincoln's confidence—as exhibited in this speech—is partially fueled by the Union Army's victory at Vicksburg, one day after Gettysburg. Citing another primary source document, namely, Lincoln's letter to Major General Meade eight days after the battle of Gettysburg, they note the historical significance of this battle as its outcome was a "missed opportunity" for the Union army because Major General Meade did not directly pursue General Lee and his army after this victory, a critique others have made of Meade's decision as it's believed that it prolonged the American Civil War. Placing this text in its historical context, the historian also notes Lincoln's intention in the speech to reunite the splintered nation while dedicating a portion of the battlefield as the Gettysburg National Cemetery.

This example illustrates the contextual nature of literacy. How we read, write, speak, listen, and represent depends on specific purposes in specific contexts. In academic disciplines, knowledge is acquired, used, and produced differently (Table 6.1).

DISCIPLINARY LITERACY INSTRUCTION

How might subject area teachers help students learn the content and the ways knowledge is acquired, used, and produced within each discipline? The field of disciplinary literacy instruction focuses on exactly this. Drawing on rhetoric studies, this relatively new body of scholarship explores how to support students in learning discipline-specific literacy skills and making explicit the ways that reading and writing are shaped by disciplinary assumptions (Fang, 2012b; Lee & Spratley, 2010; Moje, 2008; Shanahan & Shanahan, 2008; Zygouris-Coe, 2014). Because of this, conversations around adolescent literacy instruction have fundamentally shifted. More than just an argument for using specific literacy strategies with specific disciplines, a disciplinary literacy approach to literacy

Table 6.1. Subject Area Disciplinary Characteristics

Subject Area	Disciplinary Characteristics
Math	Use symbols and mathematical language.
	Develop proofs and solving problems.
	Apply mathematical concepts to real-world situations.
	Evaluate for accuracy and validity of mathematical arguments and solutions.
English Language Arts	Read, write, and critically analyze a variety of texts, including fiction and nonfiction.
	Create written works: essays, stories, poems.
	Analyze and interpret texts.
	Evaluate for the quality and coherence of written works.
Science	Experiment, observe, collect, and analyze data.
	Develop hypotheses.
	Apply scientific principles to solve problems.
	Evaluate quality and reliability of data and rigor of the scientific process.
History	Analyze primary and secondary sources, including texts, artifacts, and oral histories.
	Research, interpret, and construct narratives based on available evidence.
	Understand the social, political, and cultural contexts in which historical events occurred.
	Evaluate the accuracy and completeness of evidence and validity of the historical interpretations.
Health	Understand principles of anatomy, physiology, nutrition, physical fitness, and exercise.
	Apply principles of anatomy, physiology, and nutrition to real-world situations.
	Participate in hands-on activities such as exercise.
World Languages	Learn vocabulary, grammar, and cultural practices associated with a particular language.
	Develop listening, speaking, reading, and writing skills to communicate in a language.
	Talk or write in a given language, and analyze and interpret materials in the language (i.e., newspapers, literature).
	Use the given language to communicate effectively in real-world situations.

Table 6.1. (continued)

Subject Area	Disciplinary Characteristics
Art	Learn about different art forms, techniques, and materials.
	Learn to use and analyze visual elements such as color, line, and texture.
	Create original works of art; analyze and critique others' work.
	Evaluate composition, use of color, and overall impact.
Music	Learn about music theory, history, performance techniques, musical notation, terminology, and techniques needed to play or sing music.
	Create original compositions, analyzing musical pieces, critiquing others' work.
	Apply music theory and performance techniques to one's own performance of that of others.

instruction foregrounds the work in each field of study. It introduces and teaches students how to participate in this kind of work.

When teachers employ disciplinary literacy instruction in their classrooms, they encourage students to think, read, and function as artists, scientists, musicians, mathematicians, historians, and other specialists (Wineburg et al., 2013). It's neither possible nor reasonable for secondary teachers to know about and have experiences working in all the fields/jobs associated with their subject areas. Still, they can be intentional about using what they know about their subject and intentionally and explicitly integrate this disciplinary literacy instruction into the courses they teach. Key components of disciplinary literacy instruction include identifying, modeling, apprenticing, and scaffolding students into the language, dispositions, and ways of knowing within a discipline (Hinton & Suh, 2019; Moje, 2015; Spires et al., 2016; Wickens et al., 2015; Wolsey et al., 2019).

In a high school history class the teacher uses a primary source document to showcase how a historian reads and views the document and for what purpose. This modeling may include asking questions aloud while reading the primary source, noting information about the author, context, and intended audience. It can also involve pointing out the type of materials used to produce the artifact, noting what information this provides about the resources available and the originator(s) of the document. In contrast, in a math class, students could be reminded that mathematicians read to find specific information or concepts that they can use to solve mathematical problems. Mathematicians aren't concerned with an author's intent, the historical and cultural context of the work, or use of literary techniques. For literary scholars, however, these aspects of the text

Table 6.2. Components of Disciplinary Literacy Instruction

Disciplinary Literacy Instruction Components	Explanations
Real-World Connections	Disciplinary work is rooted in real-world issues, situations, and experiences.
	Teachers bridge students' background knowledge and experiences.
Inquiry Based	Students do the work of the discipline rather than just read about it.
	Students evaluate discipline-specific arguments, evidence, support, and claims.
	Students practice making discipline-specific arguments and claims.
	Students write or create in discipline-specific ways.
Habits of Practices are Explicitly Identified and Modeled	Explain the particular reading, writing, speaking, listening, and representing moves of the discipline.
	Explain the ways that knowledge is acquired, used, and produced in the discipline.
	Using discipline-specific texts, identify text structures, features, and language use in these texts.
	Identify and support students in learning discipline-specific vocabulary.
Collaboration	Subject area teachers can't do this work alone. Collaboration with literacy experts and in professional development is important.
	Students collaborate with one another to produce, communicate, share knowledge, and participate in disciplinary-specific practices and roles, such as problem solving.

are important because they look for deeper meaning in what they read and read for interpretation and analysis (Table 6.2).

Disciplinary literacy instruction is accessible to students at all levels because the goal is not to create experts in each discipline—scientists, historians, artists, mathematicians, literary scholars. Rather, the goals are to introduce and make explicit the ways different disciplines work and to give students experiences in creating, communicating, and producing knowledge within a particular disciplinary field. Proponents of disciplinary literacy argue that this approach to learning (i.e., content and specialized ways of interacting with the content) is needed to prepare critical thinkers who can comprehend and critique materials they encounter.

Across subject areas, disciplinary literacy instruction is important for student learning. To illustrate, rather than reading about scientific discoveries or the inquiry process, a disciplinary literacy approach focuses on doing science experiments and experiencing the inquiry process as scientists. In a biology class, students learn how to think like biologists, including the types of questions and dispositions biologists ask and maintain. These questions and lines of inquiry center on understanding and advancing knowledge connected to the natural world. Similarly, adolescents participating in marching band enhance their musical repertoire through additional study, practice, and performance. Like professional musicians, they learn to critique and enhance their own musicality while also partnering with their peers in the full ensemble to generate and perform pieces of music that audiences will enjoy. They also study composers and critiques of the pieces they learn and perform. Sometimes, they may even write, share, and perform original compositions.

In English Language Arts classes, disciplinary literacy instruction means that students learn how to analyze literary devices such as symbolism and metaphor, how to write analytical essays that support their interpretations of literary works, and how to use literary language to communicate effectively, and then use or share this learning in the kinds of texts used by members in the discipline (e.g., online book talks, book, television, and movie reviews). Students also use their knowledge of how to analyze and interpret nonfiction texts (i.e., speeches or editorials) and how to write persuasive essays that use evidence to support their arguments in response to relevant and current school, community, state-level, and national issues.

In a world language course, which focuses on students' language acquisition and cultural understanding, disciplinary literacy instruction can be used, in particular, to support students' ability to understand, appreciate, and engage in cultural practices. For example, students can access and explore multiple texts (media, social media, websites, music, etc.) to better understand the target language as well as the cultural aspects of a given language. This includes facilitating hands-on opportunities for students to practice their language skills and apply their developing cultural understanding in settings where the target language is spoken, including field trips, online resources, and direct connections with native speakers.

Across all these examples is an inquiry-based approach to learning, one that overlaps well with inquiry-based instructional approaches, including project and problem-based learning (Spires et al., 2014). We think this overlap is exciting and holds much potential across the subject areas for relevant and engaging ways to introduce disciplinary literacy, rooting the work of the discipline in real-world contexts and issues, and connecting with students' interests, expertise, and experiences.

Disciplinary Literacy: Math

Melanie started her career as an engineer and later became a math teacher. Given that she'd had a lot of practice working in the field as an engineer, she was thus uniquely positioned to incorporate disciplinary literacy instruction to help her middle school math students understand the specialized literacy practices associated with math. In a podcast episode interview with Melanie, we learned how she uses disciplinary literacy instruction with her students (Van Duinen & Hamilton, 2022). As she explains, her job is to help students learn and use math to make sense of their world, and her goal is to enable students to understand how to use math in authentic ways beyond school.

When Melanie taught her students about slope (i.e., rise over run), she also wanted them to understand how one thing changes in relation to another. While students could conceptually understand this and then apply it to problems associated with finding the slope of a line, Melanie also invited them to see how slope applies in everyday life. She wanted students to begin thinking about and solving slope problems as if they were engineers, who routinely apply the concept of rise over run, the measure of how much something changes vertically compared to how much it changes horizontally, such as when designing for wheelchair accessibility. Connected to this unit on slope, one way Melanie incorporated disciplinary literacy instruction was to challenge her students to apply engineering skills and dispositions to consider how to make their community more accessible for all people, including those with physical challenges. Part of her students' work in this unit was reading relevant portions of the Americans with Disabilities Act (ADA), accessing and reading through local building codes, and studying the ramps in their school, specifically the one in their school cafeteria.

Throughout the unit, Melanie asked students to consider the value and importance of slope and how it impacts people's everyday lives. One of the final assessments for this unit was a real-world application in which students were given a picture of someone's garage, along with relevant dimensions. With this information, Melanie's students were charged with designing a ramping system for this homeowner that met ADA slope requirements, just as an engineer would do. They also needed to ensure that the ramping system they designed maintained the garage's overall usefulness, including retaining ample space for the homeowner to park their vehicle in the garage.

As Melanie worked with students, she knew multiple solutions would meet the homeowner's needs. Ultimately, students had to present their final design and mathematical computations. They also needed to explain to Melanie and their peers how their design met the homeowner's needs while also satisfying ADA slope requirements. Not only were students able to make connections between what they were learning in Melanie's 8th-grade math class and real-world engineering tasks, they also came to understand the importance of math as it relates to people's everyday lives and needs.

Throughout these experiences, Melanie encouraged her students to problem-solve, engage in reasoning and proofs, draw connections between, communicate, and develop representations of mathematical ideas. In doing so, students not only learned math and increased their numeracy but also practiced assuming the role of an engineer, who has to balance and consider multiple factors while simultaneously identifying and creating a solution that is cost-effective, efficient, meets clients' needs, and is aesthetically appropriate for a given space.

Disciplinary Literacy: Health

Disciplinary literacy instruction in a middle school health class could look something like what we describe here. In her unit focused on middle school health and "risky substances," Holwerda (2022) designed a unit that challenged her 8th-grade students to answer the driving question, "How can we create an anti-vaping learning experience for 5th- and 6th-graders to understand the health risks and future consequences of vaping?" Part of this unit centered on students not just learning about vaping but also how to approach the topic as members of a health-related field. The end goal of the unit was for students to share their learning with younger peers while also discouraging the use of risky substances in their school. Holwerda explained in her end-of-unit reflection: "I was eager to use this for the 'risky substances' unit because it is thought to be 'all the fun things that adults don't want us to use.'" She went on to note: "I wanted THEM to dig in to [and] find the facts and also identify trusted sources and untrustworthy sources. It was a great opportunity to teach about ulterior motives and the fact that 8th-graders are actually targeted by marketers." Holwerda's students were encouraged to read and synthesize texts from the health field and share this knowledge with others.

Students read articles from health-related websites, learned discipline-specific vocabulary words, and then used this knowledge to examine marketing targeted at young adolescents, especially advertising associated with "risky substances." Based on this knowledge, students discussed together and evaluated how accurately current and past advertisements portrayed the ways these substances were intended to be ingested, inhaled, and used. Students then created their own advertisements that considered the needs of their target audience (i.e., 5th- and 6th-graders in their school) and articulated what they learned about using risky substances. Throughout this unit, students didn't just read information about vaping. They were involved in finding, making sense of, summarizing, synthesizing, and disseminating the information in their field.

Disciplinary Literacy: Social Studies

Rowe's (2022) approach to disciplinary literacy instruction was to have his 6th-grade students respond to a real-world problem in their city. Drawing on his students' knowledge of city planning, geography, and history and using the experience to deepen their understanding of social studies disciplinary questions, dispositions, and knowledge, Rowe organized a unit focused on a relevant driving question posed to him by the city manager: "How can our city change a city-owned public area to better serve its residents?"

Rowe's students partnered with the city manager, municipality staff, and city residents to examine the issue and explore four possible public locations that could be redesigned. Throughout the process, students analyzed primary and secondary sources such as city documents, artifacts, and oral histories. They constructed arguments based on evidence and reasoning and drew on many different courses of evidence for support by eliciting and considering community members' perspectives on the available public spaces. They considered cause and effect, change and continuity, and interdependence in city structures, spaces, and relationships. They proposed a solution and then communicated their ideas in various ways to stakeholders.

As noted previously, this type of teaching and learning extends students' agency (Moje, 2008), which provides access to both the accepted knowledge and practices of the discipline (e.g., roles and responsibilities of city managers). Throughout students' exploration of their community and how to best ensure that community-designed spaces actually serve its members, they also have opportunities to challenge, critique, and perhaps even shift understanding and practices. Further, by learning more about designing and redesigning community spaces, including where they and their family and friends live, Rowe's students engaged in disciplinary practices and discussions, directly enriching their understanding and skill development.

Disciplinary Literacy: Science

The use of masks during the COVID-19 pandemic was especially challenging for many individuals with hearing aids because of the way the mask straps interfered with the hearing aids and caused discomfort. Noting this issue, a middle school STEM teacher used disciplinary literacy instruction to explore with his students the question, "How might we leverage our 3D printing capabilities to make mask accessories for students with hearing aids?" Students took on the role of engineers, tasked with designing tools to support hearing-impaired individuals in wearing masks. Overway (2022) facilitated conversations between his students and a colleague's daughter who wore hearing aids, so they could better understand the challenges and needs. They used this feedback to design facemask accessory prototypes using 3D printing technology. The goal was to design mask accessories to increase comfort when wearing a mask and hearing aid simultaneously.

Students participated in the disciplinary literacy practices of consuming, creating, and critiquing knowledge in ways like those used by professionals in the field, such as engineers and 3D designers. Students also engaged in discussions using discipline-specific vocabulary, partnered with end-users, and participated in multiple rounds of design and implementation. In these ways, this unit enhanced and supported students' disciplinary literacy skills connected to understanding and engaging in discipline-specific practices associated with using engineering and 3D technology to meet a real and important need. Students were apprenticed into particular ways of thinking, knowing, understanding, and applying their knowledge.

Disciplinary Literacy Across Subject Areas

In some instances, teachers can integrate disciplinary literacy in collaboration with one or more peers across subject areas. For example, a math teacher and her history colleague decided to help their students learn more about the Electoral College during an upcoming election. We share this example for two reasons. One, it illustrates how disciplinary literacy instruction looks different across subject areas due to the specialized approaches required, as it relates to how problems, issues, challenges, and topics are approached and considered within each discipline. Second, this example demonstrates how teachers can use disciplinary literacy across subjects in collaboration to support and extend student learning. Although the learning outcomes and disciplinary literacy instruction are different within the subject areas, when students recognize explicit connections and applications in and across subject matter, learning is deeper and long-lasting.

In both subject areas, the teachers identified and practiced various discipline-specific approaches, skills, and dispositions with their students. Although both groups studied the Electoral College, their approaches, considerations, and solutions differed. While instructors used literacy strategies in each course to support students' learning (e.g., re-reading, summarizing, annotating, note-taking), the disciplinary literacy instruction differed because these aligned with the practices of the disciplines themselves. Although students examined maps, tables, and figures associated with the Electoral College, *why* and *how* they used visual data varied.

Mathematicians and statisticians look at and use numbers in particular ways for specific purposes. With this application, students saw how different formulas produce different outcomes.

The math teacher's students considered the use of proportional representation in the Electoral College related to accuracy, numbers, and calculations. The instructor supported her students in developing their mathematical thinking and numeracy. In contrast, the history teacher challenged his students to consider the history and perspectives of fairness related to the Electoral College and its outcomes, including its representation of people groups and states and when Electoral College outcomes differ from the popular vote in national elections. The instructor encouraged students to understand this particular governmental structure in light of its historical significance, including why it was conceived and adopted and how it impacts political elections and campaigning in the United States today. In doing so, this instructor supported his students' historical inquiry skill development.

Moreover, because mathematicians focus on accuracy and clarity related to the information they analyze and produce, it is important that they ensure the correctness of mathematical computations and clarity of data presentation (i.e., the findings resulting from computations associated with a particular system). As these 8th-grade math students studied and employed the mathematical formulas connected to the Electoral College, they learned how data in its raw and computed forms were used to provide information about a particular system, in this case, an election system in the United States. These students also learned, mathematically and statistically, how outcomes are directly influenced by available data and the accuracy of those data.

The 8th-grade history class students studied the Electoral College by taking the stance of historians and politicians. In this class, the disciplinary literacy instruction centered on looking at data as a story, or set of stories, to be uncovered and understood. Students were also invited to learn how to identify and consider the perspective, privilege, message, and data sources of the texts, enabling them to critically analyze and evaluate the information they studied and researched associated with the Electoral College. Historians are concerned not only with the accuracy of their data but with whose stories are foregrounded and whose stories and experiences might be under-represented or undervalued. Taking on this disciplinary approach, students concerned themselves with what the past can tell us about the present—and potentially the future.

Students studied the Electoral College to understand it, including its influence on the political parties and national election system, as well as to make sense of their own life experiences and the experiences of others, including their parents, grandparents, and friends. In the recent past, for example, there have been two national elections in which the candidate who won the popular vote did not win the electoral vote and thus did not win the overall election—even though more people voted for that candidate. While mathematicians are concerned with the accuracy of the results and understanding how the Electoral College works and is applied, mathematically speaking, historians studying the same electoral system consider and debate questions about equity, representation, access, and the impact the system has had and continues to exert on government.

In this example, these colleagues integrated disciplinary literacy instruction to support students' learning. In a math class, disciplinary literacy instruction focuses on teaching students how to read and interpret mathematical symbols and equations, how to write mathematical proofs, and how to use mathematical language to communicate effectively. Historical inquiry isn't included in a math class because it's not part of what mathematicians do. Instead, students learn how to analyze and interpret data using statistical tools. They encounter mathematical problems and learn to pose, solve, interpret, and formulate these problems in a variety of situations. Rather than interpreting primary and secondary source documents, students in math class learn to problem-solve, engage in reasoning and proofs, and draw connections between, communicate about, and develop representations of mathematical ideas.

DISCIPLINARY LITERACY INSTRUCTION IN SECONDARY SCHOOLS

Debate persists about when disciplinary literacy instruction should occur. Some argue that higher education is best suited for preparing disciplinary specialists (Heller, 2010). If it does occur at the high school level, some believe that disciplinary literacy instruction is better suited for honors or AP classes than for general or remedial classes. Some educators question if a disciplinary literacy approach is appropriate for all learners, particularly those not yet proficient in basic literacy skills, including English Learners and those who might need more support in "strategies, routines, skills, language and practices" (Faggella-Luby et al., 2012). Others take an opposite stance, arguing that disciplinary literacy instruction could and should occur at the elementary school level (Shanahan & Shanahan, 2014).

When framed with the goal of helping learners properly understand, participate in, and contribute to disciplinary conversations and knowledge, we believe a disciplinary literacy approach is needed at the secondary level. When considering the importance of student motivation and engagement in learning, disciplinary literacy instruction provides relevant and real-world connections for learning. Disciplinary literacy is important in supporting all students, not just those already proficient in speaking English.

Disciplinary Literacy Instruction Increases Access and Agency

The case studies presented above illustrate how disciplinary literacy instruction provides students access to the accepted knowledge and practices of the disciplines, allowing them to begin to critique, challenge, and perhaps even change understandings and practices. This has led to some scholars describing disciplinary literacy instruction as social justice work (Moje, 2010). Rather than just building knowledge about the disciplines, a goal of disciplinary literacy instruction is to build students' comprehension of how knowledge is traditionally produced, curated, and applied in the disciplines. This has become easier with new technologies and tools that allow the general public access to discipline-specific practices and knowledge once available only to professionals and scholars. Using these technologies and tools gives students opportunities to better understand, explore, play, and contribute to the knowledge and practices within a particular discipline.

> **INCREASED ACCESS TO DISCIPLINARY KNOWLEDGE: NEW TECHNOLOGIES**
>
> Experts in the natural and physical sciences continue to employ new technologies for modeling and studying scientific phenomena. iNaturalist, for example, is a science app that allows users to observe and identify plants, animals, and other organisms in their natural habitats. Though the app is used by biologists and ecologists to collect data and monitor changes in biodiversity, it is also available to the general public. It can be used in classrooms to help students acquire and employ this discipline-specific knowledge. In the field of history, digital archives provide historians and the general public with more access to primary documents and artifacts. As a result, historians and students have opportunities to use visual representations to generate robust and, often, more complete historical accountings. Other examples of new disciplinary-related technologies available to the general public include graphic design tools such as Canva that allow users to create professional-looking graphics and designs and health apps that help users track their diet and exercise by providing calorie and nutrient information for various foods.

Having increased access to disciplinary knowledge and being scaffolded through disciplinary literacy instruction empowers students to critically examine and question disciplinary practices. Moje (2008) argues:

> The task of literacy education, relative to these goals of learning the discourses and practices of the discipline, then becomes one of teaching students what the

privileged discourses are, when and why such discourses are useful, and how these discourses and practices came to be valued. (pp. 100–101)

Learning these discourses and practices not only helps students see how knowledge is constructed within particular disciplines but also helps them navigate among contexts. Such knowledge helps students see themselves as possible members of a discipline. In a science class, for example, students from diverse backgrounds might have varying levels of familiarity with the ways of thinking used in the discipline because of their previous experiences with science resources, their ability to encounter people in the science field, and their background knowledge. Disciplinary literacy instruction involves explicitly teaching students how to read, write, and think like scientists. In this case, it involves teaching all students the vocabulary used in the discipline as well as strategies for interpreting scientific texts and data, such as analyzing graphs and charts, establishing hypotheses, creating experiments, and critically reading scientific articles. In providing this kind of explicit support, teachers make for more equitable access to science education. They also help demystify the scientific process, claims, and knowledge through teaching the processes involved.

"YES, AND" APPROACH TO DISCIPLINARY LITERACY INSTRUCTION AND LITERACY STRATEGIES

Literacy strategies and disciplinary literacy instruction are not mutually exclusive. In the field of adolescent literacy, secondary teachers are often encouraged to use generic literacy strategies across subject areas as a way to support adolescents' literacy development. Some schoolwide initiatives identify particular literacy strategies and encourage teachers, of all subject areas, to use these strategies with their students. This approach to literacy instruction, commonly called "content area literacy," is often contrasted with a disciplinary approach, and secondary teachers can be encouraged to follow or support one or the other. Historically, this makes sense. Disciplinary literacy, as a body of research and scholarship, began in response to the perceived limitations of a content area literacy strategies approach, particularly at the secondary level.

A "yes, and" approach enables teachers to use both literacy strategies and disciplinary literacy instructional approaches. Literacy strategies can support students' learning and ability to understand discipline-specific texts and participate in disciplinary habits of practice. Teachers can highlight how and why literacy strategies might be used for different purposes, depending on the discipline. An example is the strategy of previewing a text. Readers use this strategy to recall background knowledge and set a purpose for reading. It involves skimming a text before reading and looking for various text features, such as headings or tables that might support understanding. Where disciplinary literacy instruction comes into play is that different disciplines use previewing in different ways. Historians, for example, might preview a text to learn about the author and when and where the text was written. They would then place this knowledge within the context of what was happening in the world at the time the text was written. This is different from how chemists preview texts. Chemists use previewing to try to understand what is being studied or researched. They use this knowledge to reflect on how this fits with what they already know about what is being studied and possibly to predict what might happen. Teachers should explain to students that while the literacy strategy can be used in multiple subject areas, there are different purposes and processes for using it.

As discussed in the previous chapter, employing literacy strategies across subject areas has value. In our work with beginning teachers, we emphasize the "across" and "within" when discussing both concepts. Teachers must be clear about the learning outcomes and curricular goals in their subject areas to know which literacy strategies will best support adolescents' literacy development. They know this by understanding how their discipline works. In other words, it's important to use literacy strategies to support disciplinary literacy instruction. Disciplinary literacy instruction helps teachers determine where, when, and how to use different literacy strategies. Conversely, literacy strategies can provide the important specific support needed to scaffold students into particular disciplines, including ways of being, knowing, and creating. Specific skills must be supported within the larger context of what matters in the discipline. Literacy strategies and disciplinary literacy instruction offer teachers clear, concrete, and applicable practices to implement within their own curricula and contexts.

MOVING FORWARD

Supporting adolescents' literacy development can be done in many creative ways. A "yes, and" approach to literacy instruction creates space for supporting adolescents' literacy skills through the use of specific literacy strategies while also placing the "why" of subject area learning within larger conversations of the discipline. Inviting students into the real-world work and ways of thinking and doing within a particular discipline can highlight the many ways that literacy development is ongoing and contextual. A disciplinary literacy approach also allows teachers to draw on students' own expertise and experiences.

Questions to Consider

- *What are ways you could model disciplinary habits of practice and thinking?*
- *What disciplinary-specific questions can be used to support students' learning in a unit or lesson?*
- *Connected to Chapter 3, how might you identify and draw on adolescents' experiences related to the real-world applications of a discipline?*

Conclusion

Throughout this book, we've widened the lens on adolescent literacy by exploring varied understandings of literacy, adolescents, and adolescent literacy instruction. Different adolescent literacy initiatives, programs, curricula, and professional development abound, and it can be difficult for beginning teachers to make sense of what is important, most effective, and applicable to their subject area without knowing the overall landscape or terrain of the field. A widened lens approach to adolescent literacy instruction allows us to situate various theories and ideas in a larger context. We hope this larger context propels our readers to want to learn more and dig deeper into the topics and aspects of adolescent literacy that we have touched on here.

As we've widened the lens on adolescent literacy, we've encouraged readers to assume a "yes, and" approach. It's important to know about and make sense of different initiatives, research studies, and instructional strategies. There's also power in building on these diverse ideas and theories and putting them in conversation with each other. When we do this, we expand our understanding and increase our capacity to support and serve adolescents.

In each chapter, we've focused on aspects of adolescent literacy and outlined key concepts, terms, and ideas. We identified commonly held beliefs about literacy and literacy instruction and have used these as a starting point from which to expand and consider other aspects as well. Literacy is reading, but it's more than just reading. It involves writing, speaking, viewing, listening, and representing. Reading and writing skills are central to social and economic opportunities, so supporting adolescents' reading and writing skills is important, even necessary. But it's also important to acknowledge the variety of ways in which we acquire, use, and produce knowledge.

Literacy involves general skills as well as specific skills. Fundamental literacy skills can be applied across contexts and must be taught and practiced with students. The stakes are too high not to do this. But it can be done while also recognizing important contextual factors that determine how, when, why, and with whom something is read, written, listened to, watched, or produced. Connected to this, literacy development has both finite and ongoing aspects. While we might master the skills of decoding and encoding, these skills are always situated in particular contexts that have different purposes for and ways of acquiring, using, and producing knowledge. In other words, literacy refers to more than just what happens in school. The reading, writing, speaking, listening, and representing that adolescents do in their homes, communities, and workplaces are important to them and should be to secondary teachers as well.

Adolescent literacy instruction needs to be collaborative across subject areas, multifaceted, and both skill-based and specialized. It needs to start with learning how adolescents make sense of their world through what they read, write, discuss, understand, interpret, and create. Student engagement and motivation need to be an integral part of literacy instruction, as do the unique disciplinary demands of each subject area.

KEY TAKEAWAYS: "YES, AND" CONSIDERATIONS

Taking a "yes, and" approach to adolescent literacy empowers teachers to support students' learning by focusing on specific instruction, skills, strategies, and applications and by acknowledging, understanding, and supporting adolescents' various literacy contexts. It is thus imperative that teachers attend to adolescents' literacy needs both generally and specifically, which includes the instruction, perspectives, and strategies they employ.

Literacy Is the Ability to Read and Write, Speak, Listen, and Represent

This principle informs the variety of texts teachers choose and how they use them, the variety of literacy strategies they use to support adolescents' literacy skill development, and how they introduce and invite students into disciplinary ways of thinking and doing.

Literacy Refers to General and Specific Skills

This insight helps teachers consider the support adolescents might need as they interact with complex subject area texts. Texts are written in multiple ways for a range of purposes and audiences. To successfully comprehend the texts they read, adolescents must rely on general literacy skills and learn new words and concepts, connect old and new ideas, and understand how new texts are organized.

Literacy Development Is Finite and Ongoing

This idea illuminates how teachers can support adolescents' developing literacy skills in a given subject area through the use of literacy strategies; the ways in which teachers explicitly model disciplinary-specific practices;

Conclusion

and how they consider their students' background knowledge, motivation, and engagement.

Literacy Is School, Home, and Community Based

This concept supports the need for teachers to approach, recognize, value, and integrate adolescents' interests, passions, and experiences in our subject areas.

Literacy Instruction Is the Responsibility of All Teachers

This belief informs the ways teachers think about the content in and across subject areas. Literacy strategies and disciplinary literacy instruction aren't add-ons but rather ways to support adolescents as they acquire, use, and produce content in a given subject area.

Literacy Instruction Is Multifaceted

This idea supports how literacy instruction needs to account for specific contexts and differentiated student skills and experiences. One-size-fits-all literacy initiatives that treat all adolescents, subject areas, and contexts as the same simply do not work.

Literacy Instruction Is Contextual

This insight highlights how literacy strategies and disciplinary literacy instruction are not mutually exclusive. Teaching and learning are always contextual, and literacy strategies support students' learning and ability to understand discipline-specific texts and to participate in disciplinary habits of practice.

MOVING FORWARD

Adolescence is an amazing time of life—a time in a learner's life that offers exciting opportunities. Supporting adolescents' literacy development, while not easy, offers incredible opportunities to get to know, walk alongside, and learn from adolescents, who are literate in so many ways. They can significantly contribute to the learning that needs to occur within each subject area. Widening our lens on literacy, adolescents, and adolescent literacy instruction, while drawing on a "yes, and" approach as we interact with adolescents and support their literacy development, allows us to recognize and celebrate the contributions of the dynamic, energetic, eager-to-learn young people we are fortunate to encounter in our classrooms every day.

References

Alexander, W. (2013). *Goblin secrets*. Margaret K. McElderry Books.
Alliance for Excellent Education (2018). *Adolescent literacy: Bridging the college- and career-readiness gap*. https://all4ed.org/wp-content/uploads/2016/01/FINAL-UPDATED-AEE_AdolescentLiteracy_FactSheet_May-2016.pdf
Alvermann, D. E. & Moore, D. W. (2011). Questioning the separation of in-school from out-of-school contexts for literacy learning: An interview with Donna E. Alvermann. Journal of Adolescent and Adult Literacy, 55(2): pp. 156–158. https://doi.org/10.1002/JAAL.00019
American Council on the Teaching of Foreign Languages. (2012). ACTFL performance descriptors for language learners. ACTFL. www.actfl.org/publications/guidelines-and-manuals/actfl-performance-descriptors-language-learners
An, S. (2013). Schema theory in reading. *Theory and Practice in Language Studies* 3(1), pp. 130–134. https://doi:10.4304/tpls.3.1.130–134
Aukerman, M. (2022, November 3). The science of reading and the media: Is reporting biased? Literacy Research Association. https://literacyresearchassociation.org/stories/the-science-of-reading-and-the-media-is-reporting-biased
Baker-Bell, A. (2020). *Linguistic justice: Black language, literacy, identity, and pedagogy*. Routledge. https://doi.org/10.4324/9781315147383
Barton, D., Hamilton, M., & Ivanic, R. (Eds.). (2000). Situated literacies: Theorising reading and writing in context. Routledge. https://doi.org/10.4324/9780203984963
Bear, D. R., Invernizzi, M., Templeton, S., & Johnston, F. (2016). *Words their way: Word study for phonics, vocabulary, and spelling instruction* (6th ed.). Pearson.
Beck, I. L., McKeown, M. G., & Kucan, L. (2013). *Bringing words to life: Robust vocabulary instruction* (2nd ed.). The Guilford Press.
Beers, K. (2003). *When kids can't read: What teachers can do: A guide for teachers 6–12*. Heinemann.
Biancarosa, C., & Snow, C. E. (2006). Reading next—A vision for action and research in middle and high school literacy: A report to Carnegie Corporation of New York (2nd ed.). Alliance for Excellent Education.
Bishop, R. S. (1990a). Mirrors, windows, and sliding glass doors. *Perspectives*, 6(3), ix–xi.
Bishop, R. S. (1990b). Windows and mirrors: Children's books and parallel cultures. In K. Holmes (Ed.), *Perspectives on teaching and assessing language arts* (pp. 83–92). Illinois Association of Teachers of English.
Calkins, L. M. (1986). *The art of teaching writing*. Heinemann.

Cappello, M. (2017). Considering visual text complexity: A guide for teachers. *The Reading Teacher, 70*(6), 733–739. https://doi:10.1002/trtr.1580

Career Outlook Data on Display. (2020, May). Learn more, earn more: Education leads to higher wages, lower unemployment: Career Outlook. U.S. Bureau of Labor Statistics. www.bls.gov/careeroutlook/2020/data-on-display/education-pays.htm

Cassidy, J., Grote-Garcia, S., & Ortlieb, E. (2020). What's hot in 2019: Expanded and interconnected notions of literacy. *Literacy Research and Instruction, 59*(1), 39–52. https://doi:10.1080/19388071.2019.1665786

Cassidy, J., Valadez, C. M., & Garrett, S. D. (2010). Literacy trends and issues: A look at the five pillars and the cement that supports them. *The Reading Teacher, 63*(8): 644–655. https://doi.org/10.1598/RT.63.8.3

Cervetti, G. N., Pearson, P. D., Palincsar, A. S., Afflerbach, P., Kendeou, P., Biancarosa, G., Higgs, J., Fitzgerald, M. S., & Berman, A. I. (2020). How the reading for understanding initiative's research complicates the simple view of reading invoked in the science of reading. *Reading Research Quarterly, 55*(S1), S161–S172. https://doi.org/10.1002/rrq.343

Chall, J. S. (1983). *Stages of reading development.* McGraw-Hill.

Christenbury, L., Bomer, R., & Smagorinsky, P. (2009). Introduction. In L. Christenbury, R. Bomer, & P. Smargorinsky (Eds.), *Handbook of adolescent literacy research* (pp. 3–13). Guilford Publications.

Conley, M. W. (2008). Cognitive strategy instruction for adolescents: What we know about the promise, what we don't know about the potential. *Harvard Educational Review, 78*(1), 84–108.

Cope, W., & Kalantzis, M. (2009). Multiliteracies: New literacies, new learning. *Pedagogies: An International Journal, 4*(3), 164–195. https://doi.org/10.1080/15544800903076044

Daniels, H., & Steienke, N. (2011). *Texts and lessons for content-area reading: With more than 75 articles from the New York Times, Rolling Stone, the Washington Post, Car and Driver, Chicago Tribune, and many others.* Heinemann.

Daniels, H., & Zemelman, S. (2014). *Subjects matter: Exceeding standards through powerful content-area reading.* Heinemann.

Dehaene, S. (2009). *Reading in the brain: The new science of how we read.* Penguin Books.

Dilgard, C., & Hodges, T. S. (2022). Leveraging literacy centers for phonics and fluency skill building in middle school. *The Clearing House: A Journal of Educational Strategies, Issues and Ideas, 95*(1), 7–17.

Disciplinary Literacy for Deeper Learning MOOC-Ed. (2014). *Close reading English /language arts and history/social studies.* www.youtube.com/watch?v=xoPtpdMcNcc

Draper, R. J. (2002). Every teacher a literacy teacher? An analysis of the literacy-related messages in secondary methods textbooks. *Journal of Literacy Research, 34*(3), 357–384. https://doi.org/10.1207/s15548430jlr3403_5

Dresser, R. (2012). The Impact of Scripted Literacy Instruction on Teachers and Students. *Issues in Teacher Education, 21*(1), 71–87.

Duke, N. K., & Cartwright, K. B. (2021). The science of reading progresses: Communicating advances beyond the simple view of reading. *Reading Research Quarterly, 56*(1), 25–44. https://doi.org/10.1002/rrq.411

References

Duke, N. K., Ward, A. E., & Pearson, P. D. (2021). The science of reading comprehension instruction. *Reading Teacher*, 74(6), 663–672. https://doi.org/10.1002/trtr.1993

Dweck, C. S. (2008). *Mindset: The new psychology of success*. Ballantine Books.

Ehri, L. C. (1999). Phases of development in learning to read words. In J. Oakhill & R. Beard (Eds.), *Reading development and the teaching of reading: A psychological perspective* (pp. 79–108). Blackwell Science.

Elsesser, K. (2019, December 11). Lawsuit claims SAT And ACT are biased—Here's what research says. www.forbes.com/sites/kimelsesser/2019/12/11/lawsuit-claims-sat-and-act-are-biased-heres-what-research-says/?sh=389a423c4292

Emdin, C. (2016). *For White folks who teach in the hood . . . and the rest of ya'll too: Reality pedagogy and urban education*. Beacon Press.

Faggella-Luby, M. N., Graner, P. S., Deshler, D. D., & Drew, S. V. (2012). Building a house on sand: Why disciplinary literacy is not sufficient to replace general strategies for adolescent learners who struggle. *Topics in Language Disorders*, 32(1), 69–84. https://doi.org/10.1097/TLD.0b013e318245618e

Fang, Z. (2012a). Approaches to developing content area literacies: A synthesis and a critique. *Journal of Adolescent and Adult Literacy*, 54(2), 103–108.

Fang, Z. (2012b). Language correlates of disciplinary literacy. *Topics in Language Disorders*, 32(1), 19–34.

Fisher, D., & Frey, N. (2016). *Improving adolescent literacy: Content area strategies at work* (4th ed.). Pearson.

Fisher, D., Frey, N., & Hattie, J. (2016). *Visible learning for literacy: Implementing the practices that work best to accelerate learning*. Corwin.

Fisher, D., Frey, N., & Lapp, D. (2012). *Text complexity: Raising rigor in reading*. International Reading Association.

Fisher, D., Frey, N., & Lapp, D. (2023). Veteran Teachers' understanding of "balanced literacy." *Journal of Education*, 203(1), 188–195. https://doi.org/10.1177/00220574211025980

Fleischman, P. (2013). *Seedfolks*. Harper Collins.

Flower, L., & Hayes, J. R. (1981). A cognitive process theory of writing. *College Composition and Communication*, 32(4), 365–387.

Fountas, I., & Pinnell, G. S. (2007). *The continuum of literacy learning, grades K–8: Behaviors and understandings to notice, teach, and support*. Heinemann.

Freire, P. (2000). *Pedagogy of the oppressed* (30th anniversary ed.). Continuum.

Frey, N. (2017). Characteristics of Culturally Sustaining and Academically Rigorous Classrooms. Literacy Leadership Brief.

Frey, N., Fisher, D., & Rothenberg, C. (2008). *Content-area conversations: How to plan discussion-based lessons for diverse language learners*. Association for Supervision and Curriculum Development.

Gee, J. P. (2015a). Discourse, small d, big D. In *The international encyclopedia of language and social interaction*. John Wiley & Sons, Inc. https://doi.org/10.1002/9781118611463.wbielsi016

Gee, J. P. (2015b). *Social linguistics and literacies: Ideology in discourses* (5th ed). Routledge.

Gentry, J. R., & Ouellette, G. P. (2019). *Brain words: How the science of reading informs teaching*. Stenhouse.

Gilkerson J., Richards, J. A., Warren, S. F., Montgomery, J. K., Greenwood, C. R., Kimbrough, O. D., Hansen, J. H., & Paul, T. D. (2017). Mapping the early language environment using all-day recordings and automated analysis. *American Journal of Speech-Language Pathology*, 26(2), 248–265.

Gillespie, K. (2018, October 24). How one tiny town is battling "rural brain drain." *The Hechinger Report*. https://hechingerreport.org/how-one-tiny-town-is-battling-rural-brain-drain

González, N., Moll, L., & Amanti, C. (Eds.). (2005). *Funds of knowledge: Theorizing practices in households, communities, and classrooms*. Routledge.

Goodman, K. S. (1986). *What's whole in whole language? A parent/teacher guide to children's learning*. Heinemann.

Goodman, K. S. (1989). Whole-language research: Foundations and development. *The Elementary School Journal*, 90(2), 207–221.

Gough, P., & Tunmer, W. (1986). Decoding, reading, and reading disability. *Remedial and Special Education*, 7(1), 6–10.

Graham, S., & Perin, D. (2007). Writing next: Effective strategies to improve writing of adolescents in middle and high schools—A report to Carnegie Corporation of New York. Alliance for Excellent Education. www.carnegie.org/publications/writing-next-effective-strategies-to-improve-writing-of-adolescents-in-middle-and-high-schools

Graves, M. F., & Sales, G. C. (2008). *The first 4,000 words*. Seward.

Guthrie, J. T., & Wigfield, A. (2000). Engagement and motivation in reading. In M. L. Kamil, P. B. Mosenthal, P. D. Pearson, & R. Barr (Eds.). *Reading research handbook* (Vol. III, pp. 403–424). Erlbaum.

Haas, E. M., & Brown, J. E. (2019). *Supporting English learners in the classroom*. Teachers College Press.

Harper, R. (2018). Science of adolescent learning: How body and brain development affect student learning. Alliance for Excellent Education. https://all4ed.org/wp-content/uploads/2018/08/Science-of-Adolescent-Learning-How-Body-and-Brain-Development-Affect-Student-Learning.pdf

Hattie, J. (2008). *Visible learning: A synthesis of over 800 meta analyses related to achievement*. Routledge.

Hattie, J., & Yates, G. C. R. (2013). *Visible Learning and the Science of How We Learn*. Routledge.

Heath, S. B. (1983). *Ways with words: Language, life, and work in communities and classrooms*. Cambridge University Press.

Heller, R., & Greenleaf, C.L. (2007). *Literacy instruction in the content areas: Getting to the core of middle and high school improvement*. Alliance for Excellent Education.

Heller, R. (2010). In praise of amateurism: A friendly critique of Moje's "Call for change" in secondary literacy. *Journal of Adolescent & Adult Literacy*, 54(4), pp. 267–273. https://doi.org/10.1598/JAAL.54.4.4

Hicks, T. (2021). *Mindful teaching with technology: Digital diligence in the English Language Arts, grades 6–12*. Guilford Press.

Hinchman, K. A., & Appleman, D. A. (eds.) (2017). *Adolescent literacies: A handbook of practice-based research*. Guilford Press.

References

Hinton, K., & Suh, Y. (2019). Foregrounding collaboration in disciplinary literacy: Implications from JAAL, 2008–2017. *Journal of Adolescent & Adult Literacy, 63*(3), 279–287.

Hoffman, J. V., Cabell, S. Q., Barrueco, S., Hollins, E. R., & Pearson, P. D. (2021). Critical issues in the science of reading: Striving for a wide-angle view in research. *Literacy Research: Theory, Method, and Practice, 70*(1), 87–105. https://doi.org/10.1177/23813377211032195

Holwerda, T. (2022). Big deal genius. West Michigan PBL Network. www.wmpblnetwork.org/20-ms-sci—t-holwerda.html

Hruby, G. G. (2001). Sociological, postmodern, and new realism perspectives in social constructionism: Implications for literacy research. *Reading Research Quarterly, 36*(1), 48–62. https://doi.org/10.1598/RRQ.36.1.3

Hull, G. A., & Schultz, K. (Eds.). (2002). *School's out: Bridging out-of-school literacies with classroom practice*. Teachers College Press.

Jacobs, V. A. (2008). Adolescent literacy: Putting the crisis in context. *Harvard Educational Review, 78*(1), 7–39.

Jerasa, S., & Boffone, T. (2021). BookTok 101: TikTok, digital literacies, and out-of-school reading practices. *Journal of Adolescent & Adult Literacy, 65*(3), 219–226.

Joint Committee on National Health Education Standards. (2007). *National Health Education Standards, Second Edition: Achieving Excellence*. Washington, DC: The American Cancer Society.

Kay, M. (2018). *Not light, but fire: How to lead meaningful race conversations in the classroom*. Stenhouse.

Kendi, I. X. (2019). *How to be an antiracist*. Random House.

Kim, Y. S. G. (2017). Why the simple view of reading is not simplistic: Unpacking component skills of reading using a direct and indirect effect model of reading (DIER). *Scientific Studies of Reading, 21*(4), 310–333. https://doi.org/10.1080/10888438.2017.1291643

Kirkland, D. (2011). Books like clothes: Engaging young Black men with reading. *Journal of Adolescent & Adult Literacy, 55*(3), 199–208.

Kist, W. (2013). New literacies and the common core. *Educational Leadership, 70*(6), 38–43.

Kress, G. (2010). *Multimodality: A social semiotic approach to contemporary communication*. Routledge.

Kress, G. (2016). *Learning to write* (2nd ed.). Routledge.

Krueger, E., & Christel, M. T. (2001). *Seeing & believing how to teach media literacy in the English classroom*. Heinemann.

Lankshear, C., & Knobel, M. (2007). Sampling "the new" in new literacies. In M. Knobel & C. Lankshear (Eds.), *A new literacies sampler* (pp. 1–24). Peter Lang Publishing, Inc.

Lave, J., & Wenger, E. (1991). *Situated learning: Legitimate peripheral participation*. Cambridge University Press.

Lee, C. D., & Spratley, A. (2010). *Reading in the disciplines: The challenges of adolescent literacy*. Carnegie Corporation of New York.

Lent, R. C. (2009). *Literacy for real: Reading, thinking and learning in the content areas*. Teachers College Press.

Lewis, C., Enciso, P. E., & Moje, E. B. (Eds.) (2007). *Reframing sociocultural research on literacy: Identity, agency, and power*. Routledge.

Liberman, I. Y., Shankweiler, D., & Liberman, A. M. (1989). The alphabetic principle and learning to read. In D. Shankweiler & I. Y. Liberman (Eds.), *Phonology and reading disability: Solving the reading puzzle* (pp. 1–33). University of Michigan Press.

Millar P., & Warrican S. J. (2015). Constructing a third space: Positioning students' out-of-school literacies in the classroom. In P. Smith & A. Kumi-Yeboah (Eds.), *Handbook of research on cross-cultural approaches to language and literacy development* (pp. 87–117). IGI Global.

Moje, E. B. (2002). Re-framing adolescent literacy research for new times: Studying youth as a resource. *Reading Research and Instruction*, 41(3), 211–228.

Moje, E. B. (2008). Foregrounding the disciplines in secondary literacy teaching and learning: A call for change. *Journal of Adolescent & Adult Literacy*, 52(2), 96–107. https://doi.org/10.1598/JAAL.52.2.1

Moje, E. B. (2010). *Disciplinary literacy: Why it matters and what we should do about it* [Keynote address]. National Reading Initiative 2010 Conference 2010, New Orleans, Louisiana. https://lead.nwp.org/knowledgebase/disciplinary-literacy-why-it-matters-and-what-we-should-do-about-it

Moje, E. B. (2015). Doing and teaching disciplinary literacy With adolescent learners: A social and cultural enterprise. *Harvard Educational Review*, 85(2), 254–278. https://psycnet.apa.org/doi/10.17763/0017-8055.85.2.254

Moje, E. B., & Lewis, C. (2007). *Examining opportunities to learn literacy: The role of critical sociocultural literacy research*. Routledge.

Morris, B. (2022, July 17). What a good night's sleep can do for your heart. *Wall Street Journal*. www.wsj.com/articles/what-a-good-nights-sleep-can-do-for-your-heart-11658066400

Muhammad, G. (2020). *Cultivating genius: An equity framework for culturally and historically responsive literacy*. Scholastic.

Muhammad, G. (2023). *Unearthing joy: A guide to culturally and historically responsive curriculum and instruction*. Scholastic.

Nagy, W. E., & Herman, P. A. (1987). Breadth and depth of vocabulary knowledge: Implications for acquisition and instruction. In M. G. McKeown & M. E. Curtis (Eds.), *The nature of vocabulary acquisition* (pp. 19–35). Lawrence Erlbaum Associates, Inc.

National Center for Education Statistics. (2019). *Nation's report card*. National Assessment of Educational Progress.

National Coalition for Core Arts Standards. (2014). National core arts standards. www.nationalartsstandards.org

National Council of Teachers of English (2007). *Adolescent literacy: A policy research brief*. National Council of Teachers of English. https://cdn.ncte.org/nctefiles/resources/positions/chron0907researchbrief.pdf

National Council of Teachers of English (2018). *Understanding and teaching writing: Guiding principles*. National Council of Teachers of English. https://ncte.org/statement/teachingcomposition

National Governors Association Center for Best Practices & Council of Chief State School Officers. (2010). *Common core state standards for English language *arts and literacy in history/social studies, science, and technical subjects.* Authors.

National Institute for Literacy (2007). *What content area teachers should know about adolescent literacy.* National Institute of Child Health and Human Development.

National Reading Panel. (2000). *Report of the National Reading Panel—teaching children to read: An evidence-based assessment of the scientific research literature on reading and its implications for reading instruction.* National Institute of Child Health and Human Development.

New London Group. (2000). A pedagogy of multiliteracies: Designing social futures. In B. Cope & M. Kalantzis (Eds.), *Multiliteracies: Literacy learning and the design of social futures* (pp. 9–38). Macmillan.

Nora, J., & Echevarria, J. (2016). *No more low expectations for English Language Learners.* Heinemann.

Nystrand, M. (2006). Research on the role of classroom discourse as it affects reading comprehension. *Research in the Teaching of English, 40*(4), 392–412.

O'Brien, D. G., Stewart, R. A., & Moje, E. B. (1995). Why content literacy is difficult to infuse into the secondary school: Complexities of curriculum, pedagogy, and school culture. *Reading Research Quarterly, 30*(3), 442–463.

Orwell, G. (2021). *Politics and the English language.* Renard Press Ltd.

Overway, I. (2022). 3D Printing and mask accessories. West Michigan PBL Network. www.wmpblnetwork.org/20-ms—stem-i-overway.html

Paris, D. (2012). Culturally sustaining pedagogy: A needed change in stance, terminology, and practice. *Educational Researcher, 41*(3), 93–97. https://doi.org/10.3102/0013189X12441244

Paris, D., & Alim, H. S. (2017). *Culturally sustaining pedagogies: Teaching and learning for justice in a changing world.* Teachers College Press.

Park, L. S. (2010). *A long walk to water.* Clarion Books.

Patterson, A., Roman, D., Friend, M., Osborne, J., & Donovan, B. (2018) Reading for meaning: The foundational knowledge every teacher of science should have. *International Journal of Science Education, 40*(3), 291–307. https://doi:10.1080/09500693.2017.1416205

Pearson, P. D. (2004). The reading wars. *Educational Policy, 18*(1), 216–252.

Pearson, P. D., & Gallagher, M. C. (1983). The instruction of reading comprehension. *Contemporary Educational Psychology, 8*(3), 317–344.

Pories, M. J. (2014). *Yes, and! Harnessing the power of improvisation to transform your life and work.* Fishladder Press.

Pressley, T., Allington, R. L., & Pressley, M. (2023). *Reading instruction that works: The case for balanced teaching* (5th ed.). Guilford Press.

Price-Dennis, D., & Muhammad, G. E. (2021). *Black girls' literacies: Transforming lives and literacy practices.* Routledge.

Purcell-Gates, V., Jacobson, E., & Degener, S. (2004). *Print literacy development: Uniting cognitive and social practice theories.* Harvard University Press.

Quigley, A. (2018). *Closing the vocabulary gap.* Routledge.

RAND Reading Study Group (2002). Reading for understanding: Toward a research and development program in reading comprehension. Office of Education Research and Improvement.

Robinson, G. C., & Norton, P. C. (2019). A decade of disproportionality: A state-level analysis of African American students enrolled in the primary disability category of speech or language impairment. *Language, Speech, and Hearing Services in Schools, 50*(2), 267–282. https://doi.org/10.1044/2018_LSHSS-17-0149

Rowe, B. (2022). A fresh look for the city of Holland. West Michigan PBL Network. www.wmpblnetwork.org/20-ms-civics—brent-rowe.html

Salinger, T. (2011). Addressing the "crisis" in adolescent literacy. *American Institutes for Research*. www2.ed.gov/programs/slcp/finalcrisis.pdf

Salinsky, T., & Frances-White, D. (2017). *The improv handbook: The ultimate guide to improvising in comedy, theatre, and beyond* (2nd ed.). Bloomsbury.

Salmerón, L., & Llorens, A. (2019). Instruction of digital reading strategies based on eye-movements modeling examples. *Journal of Educational Computing Research, 57*(2), 343–359. https://doi.org/10.1177/0735633117751605

Sarigianides, S. T., Petrone, R., & Lewis, M. A. (2017). *Rethinking the "adolescent" in adolescent literacy*. National Council of Teachers of English.

Sciurba, K. (2014). Texts as mirrors, texts as windows: Black adolescent boys and the complexities of textual relevance. *Journal of Adolescent and Adult Literacy, 58*(4), 308–316. https://doi:10.1002/jaal.358

Sedita, J. (2013). Learning to write and writing to learn. In Hougen, M. (Ed.). *Fundamentals of literacy instruction & assessment: 6–12*. Paul H. Brookes.

Seidenberg, M. (2017). *Language at the speed of sight: How we read, why so many can't, and what can be done about it*. Basic Books.

Serafini, F., & Gee, E. (2017). *Remixing multiliteracies: Theory and practice from New London to new times*. Teachers College Press.

Shanahan, T. (2005). *The National Reading Panel Report. Practical Advice for Teachers*. Learning Point Associates/North Central Regional Educational Laboratory (NCREL).

Shanahan, T., & Shanahan, C. (2008). Teaching disciplinary literacy to adolescents: Rethinking content-area literacy. *Harvard Educational Review, 78*(1), 40–59. https://doi.org/10.17763/haer.78.1.v62444321p602101

Shanahan, T., & Shanahan, C. (2012). What is disciplinary literacy and why does it matter? *Topics in Language Disorders, 32*(1), 7–18. https://doi.org/10.1097/TLD.0b013e318244557a

Shanahan, C., & Shanahan, T. (2014). Does disciplinary literacy have a place in elementary school? *The Reading Teacher, 67*(8), 636–639. https://doi:10.1002/trtr.1257

Shipp, J. (2017). *The grown-up's guide to teenage humans: How to decode their behavior, develop trust, and raise a respectable adult*. Brilliant Partners.

Simon, R., & Kalan, A. (2017). Adolescent literacy and collaborative inquiry. In K. A. Hinchman & D. A. Appleman (Eds.), *Adolescent literacies: A handbook of practice-based research* (pp. 398–420). Guilford Press.

Snow, C. E., Porche, M. V., Tabors, P. O., & Harris, S. R. (2007). *Is literacy enough? Pathways to academic success for adolescents*. Paul H. Brookes.

Sparks, S. D. (2022, October 24). Two decades of progress, nearly gone: National math, reading scores hit historic lows. *Education Week*. www.edweek.org/leadership/two-decades-of-progress-nearly-gone-national-math-reading-scores-hit-historic-lows/2022/10

Sperry, D. E., Sperry, L. L., & Miller, P. J. (2019). Reexamining the verbal environments of children from different socioeconomic backgrounds. *Child Development*, *90*(4), 1303–1318.

Spires, H. A., Kerkhoff, S. N., & Graham, A. C. K. (2016). Disciplinary literacy and inquiry: Teaching for deeper content learning. *Journal of Adolescent and Adult Literacy*, *60*(2), 151–161. https://doi:10.10002/jaal.577

Spires, H. A., Kerkhoff, S., Graham, A., & Lee, J. (2014). *Relating inquiry to disciplinary literacy: A pedagogical approach*. Friday Institute for Educational Innovation.

Street, B. V. (1995). *Social literacies*. Longman.

Street, B. V. (2001). *Literacy and development: Ethnographic perspectives*. Routledge. https://doi.org/10.4324/9780203468418

Suleiman, A. B., & Dahl, R. E. (2017). Leveraging neuroscience to inform adolescent health: The need for an innovative transdisciplinary developmental science of adolescence. *Journal of Adolescent Health*, *60*(3), 240–248. https://doi.org/10.1016/j.jadohealth.2016.12.010

Swanson, E., Vaughn, S., & Wexler, J. (2017). Enhancing adolescents' comprehension of text by building vocabulary knowledge. *Teaching Exceptional Children*, *50*(2), 84–94.

Taboada, A., Tonks, S. M., Wigfield, A., & Guthrie, J. T. (2009). Effects of motivational and cognitive variables on reading comprehension. *Reading and Writing*, *22*(1), 85–106. http://dx.doi.org/10.1007/s11145-008-9133-y

Troyer, M. (2017). A mixed-methods study of adolescents' motivation to read. *Teachers College Record*, *119*(5), 1–48. https://doi.org/10.1177/016146811711900502

Turner, K. H., & Hicks, T. (2015). *Argument in the real world: Teaching adolescents to read and write digital texts*. Heinemann.

Vance, J. D. (2016). *Hillbilly elegy: A memoir of a family and culture in Crisis*. HarperCollins.

Van Duinen, D. V., & Hamilton, E. R. (hosts). (2022). Disciplinary literacy in Math with Melanie Dever (Season Two, Episode 6). [Audio podcast episode]. In All About Literacy. https://open.spotify.com/episode/6p0UaM6DqqaXVzT5n2OvtB?si=2f63b85a49544fd7

Vernon, J. A., Trujillo, A., Rosenbaum, S., & DeBuono, B. (2007). Low health literacy: Implications for national health policy. Health Sciences Research Commons. Washington, DC: George Washington University. http://hsrc.himmelfarb.gwu.edu/sphhs_policy_facpubs/172

Vygotsky, L. S. (1978). *Mind in society: The development of higher psychological processes*. Harvard University Press.

Wharton-McDonald, R., Pressley, M., & Hampston, J. (1998). Literacy instruction in nine first-grade classrooms: Teacher characteristics and student achievement. *Elementary School Journal*, *99*(2), 103–119.

Wickens, C. M., Manderino, M., Parker, J., & Jung, J. (2015). Habits of practice: Expanding disciplinary literacy frameworks through a physical education lens. *Journal of Adolescent & Adult Literacy*, *59*(1), 75–82. https://doi.org/10.1002/jaal.429

Wiggins, G. P., & McTighe, J. (2005). *Understanding by design*, (2nd ed.). ASCD.

Willingham, D. T. (2015). *Raising kids who read: What parents and teachers can do*. Jossey-Bass.

Willingham. D., & Lovette, G. (2014). Can reading comprehension be taught? *Teachers College Record*. www.tcrecord.org.proxy.its.virginia.edu

Wineburg, S. S. (2001). *Historical thinking and other unnatural acts: Charting the future of teaching the past*. Temple University Press.

Wineburg, S. S., Martin, D., & Monte-Sano, C. (2013). *Reading like a historian: Teaching literacy in middle and high school history classrooms*. Teachers College Press.

Winn, M. T. (2011). *Girl time: Literacy, justice, and the school-to-prison pipeline*. Teachers College Press.

Winter, J. (2022, September 1). The rise and fall of vibes-based literacy. The New Yorker. www.newyorker.com/news/annals-of-education/the-rise-and-fall-of-vibes-based-literacy

Wolf, M. (2008). *Proust and the squid: The story and science of the reading brain*. Harper Collins.

Wolsey, T. D., Lapp, D., Grant, M. C., & Karkouti, I. M. (2019). Intersections of literacy and teaching with the disciplines and professions: We asked some experts. *Journal of Adolescent & Adult Literacy, 63*(3), pp. 251–256. https://www.jstor.org/stable/48556209

Woodson, J. (2015). *Locomotion*. Puffin Books.

World Health Organization (2023). *Adolescent health*. www.who.int/health-topics/adolescent-health#tab=tab_1

Wyse, D., & Bradbury, A. (2022). Reading wars or reading reconciliation? A critical examination of robust research evidence, curriculum policy and teachers' practices for teaching phonics and reading. *Review of Education, 10*(1), 1–53. https://doi.org/10.1002/rev3.3314

Zygouris-Coe, V. (2014). *Teaching discipline-specific literacies in grades 6–12: Preparing students for college, career, and workforce demands*. Routledge.

Index

Academic literacy, 45, 51–53
Adolescence, definitions of, 7, 10–12
Adolescent literacy
  contextual aspects, 53–59
  overview and definitions, 2, 13–14
  skill development, 83–93
  See also Literacy
African American studies, AP curriculum, 51
Alexander, William, 86, 87
Alim, H. S., 50
Alliance for Excellent Education, 10, 11
Alvermann, Donna, 19
American Council on the Teaching of Foreign Languages (ACTFL), 65
Americans with Disabilities Act (ADA), 106–107
An, S., 38
Appalachian English, 52
Appleman, D. A., 16
Apprenticeship model of learning, 48
Appropriation, avoidance of, 58–59
Asset-based approaches, 12, 53, 54
Aukerman, M., 29

Background knowledge, 27, 29, 37–38, 85
Baker-Bell, A., 50, 51, 52, 58
Balanced literacy approach, 30
Barton, D., 46
Bear, D. R., 39
Beck, I. L., 36, 87
Beers, K., 85
Biancarosa, C., 1
Bishop, R. S., 75
Black English, 52, 53

Boffone, T., 56
Bradbury, A., 29
Brown, J. E., 80

Calkins, L. M., 30
Cappello, M., 73
Career Outlook Data on Display, 1
Cartwright, K. B., 37
Cassidy, J., 33
Cervetti, G. N., 37
Chall, J. S., 32
Christel, M. T., 72
Christenbury, L., 45, 53, 57
Close reading, 23, 95
  of Gettysburg Address, 100–101
Common Core State Standards (CCSS), 65–66
Comprehension, 27, 37
Conley, M. W., 23
Content area literacy, 79, 83, 85, 113
Contextual aspects of literacy, 45–53
  adolescent literacy, 53–59
Cope, W., 62
Cultural appropriation, 58–59
Cultural background of students, 52–53

Dahl, R. E., 11
Daniels, H., 88, 90
Dehaene, S., 28
Dilgard, C., 22
Directed Reading Thinking Activities, 85–86
Disciplinary literacy, 99–100
  across subject areas, 109–111
  English Language Arts, 100–101, 105

Disciplinary literacy (*continued*)
   health, 107–108
   math, 106–107
   science, 108–109
   secondary school instruction, 111–113
   social studies, 100–101, 108
Disciplinary Literacy for Deeper Learning MOOC-Ed, 100
Discourse, literacy as, 49
Discussion strategies, 90–92, 95
Double-Entry Journal strategy, 85–86
Draper, R. J., 85
Dresser, R., 23
Duke, N. K., 29, 37
Dweck, C. S., 3, 43, 53

Echevarria, J., 53, 80
Ehri, L. C., 32
Electoral College, cross-disciplinary example, 109–111
Elsesser, K., 18
Emdin, C., 22, 50, 51, 52
Engagement, 24, 41–42, 44, 76, 118
English Language Arts disciplinary literacy, 100–101, 105
English learners, 33, 36, 43, 52–53, 68, 80, 111
Exit tickets, 95

Faggella-Luby, M. N., 111, xii
Fang, Z., 8, 101
Fawcett, Eliza, 51
Fisher, D., 23, 24, 30, 68, 79–80, 96
Fleischman, Paul, 86
Flower, L., 39
Fluency, 27, 32, 34–35
Fountas, I., 30
Frances-White, D., 4
Frayer model, 88
Freire, P., 8
Frey, N., 75, 90

Gallagher, M. C., 94
Gee, J. P., 16, 45, 46, 49, 50
Gentry, J. R., 18, 31
Gettysburg Address, close reading of, 100–101
Gillespie, K., 71

Goblin Secrets (Alexander), 86, 87
González, N., 48, 53
Goodman, K. S., 29
Gough, P., 37
Graham, S., 1
Graphic organizers, 87, 88, 95
Graves, M. F., 35
Greenleaf, C. L., 1
Guthrie, J. T., 41

Haas, E. M., 80
Hamilton, E. R., 106
Harper, R., 10
Hartocollis, Anemona, 51
Hattie, J., 96
Hayes, J. R., 39
Health
   disciplinary literacy, 107–108
   writing strategies, 89–90
Heath, S. B., 48, 50
Heller, R., 1, 111
Herman, P. A., 35
Hicks, T., 16, 92
Hillbilly Elegy (Vance), 71
Hinchman, K. A., 16
Hinton, K., 103
History writing strategies, 89
Hodges, T. S., 22
Hoffman, J. V., 29
Holwerda, T., 107
Hruby, G. G., 46
Hull, G. A., 19, 45, 48

Inquiry-based learning, 100, 105–106

Jacobs, V. A., 1
Jerasa, S., 56
Jigsaw strategy, 85–86

Kalan, A., 13
Kalantzis, M., 62
Kay, M., 51, 52
Kendi, I. X., 51, 52, 58
Kim, Y. S. G., 37
Kirkland, D., 42
Kist, W., 71
Knobel, M., 50
Kress, G., 39, 61

Index

Krueger, E., 72
KWL (Know, Want to Know, Learned) chart strategy, 83

Lankshear, C., 50
Lave, J., 48
layering texts, 74
Lee, C. D., 101
Lent, R. C., 42
Lewis, C., 47, 49, 50
Liberman, I. Y., 39
Literacy
  academic, 45, 51–53
  beliefs about, 14–24
  contextual aspects, 45–53, 119
  literacy strategies, 79, 83–93
  overview, 7–9, 118–119
  reading skills, 31–38
  skill development, 79–83
  statistics, 1
  theories of, 2–3
  widened lens metaphor, 3–5, 117
  writing skills, 39–41
  See also Adolescent literacy; Disciplinary literacy; Literacy instruction
Literacy instruction
  balanced literacy approach, 30
  disciplinary instruction in secondary schools, 111–113
  disciplinary literacy, 101–106
  literacy strategies, 93–96
  motivation and engagement, 41–42
  overview, 9–10
  science of reading approach, 28–29
  students who struggle, 42–43
  texts, use of, 73–76
  whole-language approach, 29–30
Llorens, A., 92
Locomotion (Woodson), 86
A Long Walk to Water (Park), 86
Lovette, G., 95
Luke, A., xi

Math
  disciplinary literacy, 106–107
  vocabulary strategies, 88
McTighe, J., 94

Millar, P., 51, 52
Miller, P. J., 35
Mind Mapping strategies, 92
Moje, E. B., xi, 19, 47, 48, 101, 103, 108, 112–113
Moore, D. W., 19
Morris, B., 70
Motivation, 24, 41–42, 44
Muhammad, G., 50, 52, 53, 54, 56–57, 58, 74

Nagy, W. E., 35
National Center for Education Statistics, 1
National Core Arts Standards (NCAS), 65
National Council of Teachers of English (NCTE), 14, 19, 41
National Health Education Standards, 94
National Institute for Literacy, 1
National Reading Panel, 32–33
New London Group, 62
Night (Wiesel), 68
Non-print-based texts, 71–73
Nora, J., 53, 80
Norton, P. C., 53
Nystrand, M., 90

O'Brien, D. G., 99
Orwell, G., 67
Ouellette, G. P., 18, 31
Overway, I., 109

Paris, D., 50
Park, Linda Sue, 86
Patterson, A., 38
Pearson, P. D., 28, 29, 94
Pedagogy, 2, 4, 7, 13–14
Perin, D., 1
Phonemic awareness, 33–34, 35, 39
Phonics, 29–30, 34
Pinnell, G. S., 30
Pories, M. J., 4
Practice
  adolescent literary contexts, 53–60
  definitions, 7
  historical and current, 50–51

Practice (*continued*)
  outside of school contexts, 48
  pedagogy and, 13–14
  research-informed, 21–22
Pressley, T., 29
Price-Dennis, D., 52
Primary source documents, 16–17, 101, 103–104
Print Literacy Development (Purcell-Gates et al.), 3
Proximal development, zone of, 47
Purcell-Gates, V., 3

Question-Answer Relationship strategy, 85–86
Questions to ask students to understand contexts, 55–56

RAND Reading Study Group, 37, 71
Readability formulas, 66–67
Reader and task considerations, 70–71
Reading initiatives, secondary school, 23
Reading in the Brain (Dehaene), 28
Reading skills
  comprehension, 37
  fluency, 34–35
  phonemic awareness, 33–34
  phonics, 34
  vocabulary, 35–36
Reading strategies, 85–87
Robinson, G. C., 53
Rowe, B., 108

Sales, G. C., 35
Salinger, T., 1
Salinsky, T., 4
Salmerón, L., 92
Sarigianides, S. T., 12
Schoolwide strategy implementation, 21, 82–83
Schultz, K., 19, 45, 48
Science disciplinary literacy, 108–109
Science of reading approach, 28–29
Sciurba, K., 75
Secondary schools
  disciplinary literacy instruction, 111–113
  reading initiatives, 23

Sedita, J., 40
Seedfolks (Fleischman), 86
Seidenberg, M., 31–32
Serafini, F., 16
Shanahan, C., xii, 99, 101, 111
Shanahan, T., xii, 33, 99, 101, 111
Shipp, J., 11
Simon, R., 13
Skateboarding as skill acquisition example, 48
Snow, C. E., 1, 35
Social media, 18, 47, 56, 59–60, 74
Social studies
  disciplinary literacy, 100–101, 108
  history writing strategies, 89
Sociocultural theory, 46–47, 57
Socratic Seminars, 90
Southern American English, 52
Sparks, S. D., 1, 18
Sperry, D. E., 35
Sperry, L. L., 35
Spires, H. A., 103, 105
Spratley, A., 101
Steienke, N., 90
Street, B. V., 46, 48
"Struggling" students, 27, 33, 42–43
Suh, Y., 103
Suleiman, A. B., 11
Swanson, E., 35

Taboada, A., 41
Talk and Turn discussions, 90
Talk stems, 90–92
Technology, digital, 16, 112
  social media, 56
Texts
  definitions, 61
  identifying texts, 61–64
  instructional uses, 73–76
  layering texts, 74
  non-print-based, 71–73
  power, privilege, and text selection, 75–76
  print-based, 65–71
  text complexity, 61, 64–65
  text selection, questions to consider, 77

Index

Think-Pair-Share discussions, 90, 95
3D printing, 109
Troyer, M., 41
Tunmer, W., 37
Turner, K. H., 92

Vance, J. D., 71
Van Duinen, D. V., 106
Vernon, J. A., 1
Visual strategies, 92–93
Vocabulary, 27, 35–36, 87–88
Vygotsky, Lev, 47–48

Warrican, S. J., 51, 52
Wenger, E., 48
Wharton-McDonald, R., 30
Whole-language approach, 29–30
Wickens, C. M., 99, 103
Widened lens metaphor for literacy, 3–5, 117
Wiesel, Elie, 68
Wigfield, A., 41
Wiggins, G. P., 94
Willingham, D. T., 31, 32, 95
Wineburg, S. S., 99, 103

Winn, M. T., 1
Winter, J., 30
Wolf, M., 32
Wolsey, T. D., 103
Woodson, Jacqueline, 86
Word Walls, 87, 94–95
World Health Organization, 10
Writing skills, 39–41
    teaching strategies, 88–90
Wyse, D., 29

Yates, G. C. R., 96
"Yes, and" approaches
    across subject areas, 96
    beliefs, commonly held, new concepts for, 14–24
    literacy contexts and practices, 59–60
    literacy instruction, 113–114
    overview of concept, 4, 118–119
    reading and writing skills, 43–44
    texts, identifying and using, 76

Zemelman, S., 88
Zygouris-Coe, V., 101

About the Authors

Deborah Vriend Van Duinen is the Arnold and Esther Sonneveldt Professor of Education at Hope College in Holland, Michigan. She previously worked as a high school teacher.

Erica R. Hamilton is a former secondary educator and currently serves as an Assistant Vice President for Academic Affairs and Associate Professor of Literacy Studies at Grand Valley State University in Allendale, Michigan.